I0627063

Principles of Biblical Christianity

The Commonly Unknown Jewels of the Bible

Kouakou E. Diby, PhD

ISBN Paperback ISBN 979-8-9932281-1-2
ISBN Hardback: ISBN 979-8-9932281-2-9
ISBN Ebook: ISBN 979-8-9932281-0-5

TABLE OF CONTENTS

Acknowledgments

Introduction...7

Chapter 1 – Motivation: Counting the Cost
  of Discipleship 9

Chapter 2 – Faith: Defining the Essence of Christianity 13

Chapter 3 – Love: The Divine Purpose for Mankind 23

Chapter 4 – Created Free, Predestined to Glory 27

Chapter 5 – Predestination: The Divine Redemptive Plan
  for Mankind 35

Chapter 6 – Sin: Mankind's Misguided Exercise
  of Free Will 51

Chapter 7 – Salvation: Restoring Mankind's Lost
  Divine Image...63

Chapter 8 – A House Built on Sand....................................77

Chapter 9 – Walking the Talk 83

Chapter 10 – Spiritual Gifts and Christian Ministry...........109

Chapter 11 – The Achilles Heel..125

Conclusion 137

ACKNOWLEDGMENTS

It took me many years of studying the Bible and prayer to complete this book. I could not have done it without the support and encouragement of my family.

To my dear sweetheart, Paulette Diby, the love of my life, thank you for dedicating your time and effort to reading and critiquing the manuscript throughout the process.

To my dear granddaughter Mado Grahouri, thank you for your detailed review and feedback that brought a millennial perspective to the book.

To my children—Emeline and her husband, Deogratias, Eve-Amable, Yannis-Elchanan, and Elanisa-Anaya—thank you for reviewing the manuscript, contributing a Gen Z perspective, and supporting me in the process.

INTRODUCTION

I never imagined I would be writing a Christian book, but the more I thought about how far many churches around the world have strayed from biblical Christianity, the more compelled I felt to speak out.

I was born and raised in a Christian family that faithfully attended an evangelical church, where my father dedicated most of his life to ministry and leadership until the Lord took him home in 1995. On one hand, I sang in choirs from the age of 10; I was baptized at 14, regularly attended Sunday school, and listened to countless sermons, which raised many questions in my young, inquisitive mind. I should note that I was baptized at least three times by different churches I attended over the years.

On the other hand, I committed my share of trespasses and transgressions, perceiving God primarily as my parents' God, but the Lord was gracious and turned me around in due time. During the early '90s, I was blessed with the teaching and example of a pastor and good friend who trained me to study biblical texts and search for answers in the Scriptures. Twenty years later, through diligent and prayerful study, the Holy Spirit opened my mind to understand the biblical answers to my long-standing questions.

Having since met countless professing Christians who have yet to be enlightened in some foundational biblical truths, I felt compelled by the Holy Spirit to write this book to share with those who may still be seeking answers, with the purpose of edifying the body of Christ. These truths are invaluable to those who need to make the life-changing decision to become Christians. They are equally valuable to those who have made that decision without fully understanding what it means to be a disciple of Christ; for how can we know that we have *faith* if we do not understand what *faith* is? How can we know that we *believe in* Christ if we don't understand what it means to *believe in* Him?

My prayer is that in the next few chapters of this book, we will examine together, through pertinent Scriptures, some of these foundational truths and effectively build assurance of our lives in Christ along the way. May the Holy Spirit tune our minds to understand, open our spiritual eyes to see, and strengthen our faith to embrace and abide in His life-changing revelations.

CHAPTER 1

MOTIVATION

Counting the Cost of Discipleship

Which of you, intending to build a tower, does not sit down first and count the cost, whether he has enough to finish it— lest, after he has laid the foundation, and is not able to finish, all who see it begin to mock him, saying, 'This man began to build and was not able to finish.' Or what king, going to make war against another king, does not sit down first and consider whether he is able with ten thousand to meet him who comes against him with twenty thousand? Or else, while the other is still a great way off, he sends a delegation and asks conditions of peace. (Luke 14:28-32 NKJV)

In these words, the Lord Jesus Christ explained the seriousness and clarity of thought needed before making the solemn decision to become His disciple (a Christian). He emphasizes the prospective disciple's need to "sit down first and count the cost" of Christian discipleship. His words not only indicate that deciding whether or not to become a Christian is very serious, but they also convey the responsibility of the prospective Christian to fully understand what is at stake. Indeed, it is the most important choice of a lifetime, leading to eternal life in God's presence or eternal damnation in hell, forever separated from God.

Most of us have had ample opportunities to make critical, even life-changing decisions. The process often involves earnest information gathering, analysis of the benefits and drawbacks of each available option, and trade-offs between competing alternatives.

An intimate understanding of the important facts and their relationships to each other is developed throughout this process. In the end, a reassuring insight into the matter at hand emerges, guiding the choice of the most beneficial and least detrimental alternative.

The stakes could not be higher when it comes to deciding one's eternal destiny. The Bible teaches that every human being who has ever lived possesses an everlasting soul. It also teaches that our world, as we know it, will pass away at some point in the future, and the soul of every person who has ever died will be reunited with his or her body, just as Jesus Christ's soul and body were reunited when He rose from the dead (Mark 16:1-7). Therefore, it is not a matter of *if,* but *when* each of us will come face-to-face with our individually chosen eternal destiny. No one shall escape; not explicitly choosing to follow Jesus Christ is, in His eyes, a choice against Him (Matthew 12:30).

As serious as this decision is, many of us decided to become Christians without truly understanding what was at stake. Perhaps we were in church and heard a preacher promise a trouble-free life, financial prosperity, or guaranteed success in whatever ways we imagined. Maybe we were compelled by life circumstances to heed those words with no other way out. Whatever our motivation, unless we had already been taught the complete biblical truth about what it means to follow Jesus, we may have "jumped on the bandwagon" without fully understanding the gospel of God's grace and mercy. Thus, it could not have been a grateful acceptance of the gift of eternal life.

Many of us spend several years, even decades, going through the motions without knowing what it truly means to be a Christian. Perhaps we think we are strong Christians because we sing or play instruments in the worship band. Or we believe so because we associate with others who also profess to be Christians. Maybe we regularly attend Bible study or small group gatherings. Better yet, we know the Bible well and can recite entire passages. We can speak the Christian jargon of the day, or hold positions such as deacon, elder, or pastor. So how could we not be Christians?

Well, the answer lies primarily in the motives that drive us. No self-serving motivations should compete with our devotion to Christ. You might ask: what do you mean? So I owe you a little more explanation.

Consider these words of Jesus recorded in Matthew 7:21-23:

11

Not everyone who says to Me, 'Lord, Lord,' shall enter the kingdom of heaven, but he who does the will of My Father in heaven. Many will say to Me in that day, 'Lord, Lord, have we not prophesied in Your name, cast out demons in Your name, and done many wonders in Your name?' And then I will declare to them, 'I never knew you; depart from Me, you who practice lawlessness! (NKJV)

In this passage, the Lord Jesus is not denying the claims made by those engaged in the conversation with Him. Indeed, they may very well have performed all the wonders they are asserting as proof of their high status in Christian circles. However, the context of the passage suggests that the charge the Lord is making against them is hypocrisy. They did things publicly, claiming to do so "in the name of the Lord," while their true motivations and hearts were far from His cause. In other words, their deeds were driven by selfish ambitions, not by faith in Jesus Christ. Since faith is the very foundation of our relationship with Him, we must understand what it truly means. What is faith? Our discussion of the principles of biblical Christianity would not be complete without addressing this question, which leads us into our first topic of study: faith.

CHAPTER 2

FAITH

Defining the Essence of Christianity

Most, if not all, people familiar with Scripture agree that faith is of paramount importance in Christianity. In fact, faith is so central to Christianity that I would argue it becomes a futile human endeavor without it. However, do not take my word for it; read what Hebrews 11:6 says: "Without faith it is impossible to please Him, for he who comes to God must believe that He is, and that He is a rewarder of those who diligently seek Him" (NKJV). Thus, the following question warrants a biblical answer for the inquisitive mind: what is faith? Does the word "faith" as used in the ancient biblical text carry the same meaning as it does today?

In John 3:16, Jesus said: "For God so loved the world that He gave His only begotten Son, that whoever believes in Him should not perish but have everlasting life" (NKJV). Is belief the same as faith? To make matters more confusing, the Lord's statement in John 3:36 reads: "And anyone who believes in God's Son has eternal life. Anyone who doesn't obey the Son will never experience eternal life but remains under God's angry judgment" (NLT). What does obedience have to do with faith or belief?

These are a few of the fundamental questions I pondered for many years in my quest to understand the essence of my life as a Christian. In seeking answers, I realized that faith is much more than simple belief. It is the foundation of the Christian life. Let us explore this further.

Saving Faith: The Defining Characteristic of True Christians
Believing is to have faith, and to have "faith is to obey regardless of consequence."

As unequivocally conveyed in the Gospel of John 3:16 and 14:6, *belief in* Jesus Christ is the only way of salvation provided by God's unfailing love for mankind. For that reason alone, the prospective Christian must understand what it means to believe in Christ. Note that in John 3:16, the Lord Jesus Christ did not say whoever believes *Him* shall not perish, but rather "that whoever believes **in** Him should not perish." One might ask: what is the difference in nuance between believing something or someone versus believing *in* something or someone? In the context of Christianity, the difference could not be greater: it means eternal life or eternal death.

Believing someone or something is an intellectual assent to the veracity of a fact about that individual or thing. For example, a young African schoolboy who has learned in school about the Great Wall of China comes to accept its existence as truth. The truth of that fact has no immediate impact and may never bear any relevance to the youngster's life. In contrast, we read in James 2:19-20, "You believe that there is one God. You do well. Even the demons believe—and tremble!" (NKJV).

There is nothing wrong with intellectually assenting to the truth of the existence of one true God. James is simply making the point that such an intellectual assent is utterly insufficient when it comes to Christian discipleship. Likewise, acceptance of facts about Jesus Christ as truths makes no difference for anyone regarding heaven or hell. Clearly, John 3:16 signifies more than an intellectual assent to the veracity of facts about Jesus Christ.

To "believe in" is a term that exists in languages other than Hebrew and Greek, in which the original Bible text was written. My own native African dialect—Baoulé—uses an expression, which translated into English would read "to sleep on," to convey belief in someone or something.

Centuries ago, my ancestors were mostly hunters who spent several days and nights hunting in the African jungle. Choosing a place to sleep for the night was not a trivial exercise. They would only sleep in a place deemed safe and secure—a place they trusted with their well-being while they slept, totally unaware of their surroundings. The significance of this expression is that it conveys total trust, even concerning life and death. Granted, they would not even consider sleeping in such a place if they did not believe some security facts about it, but it takes more than acceptance of such facts to surrender one's well-being to the safety and security of that place.

Perhaps a discourse of "belief in" in terms of a practical, real-life event shall help us shed more light on its meaning.

Figure 1: Blondin, crossing the Niagara Falls with his manager on the back

Most historians remember Jean-François Gravelet's historic tight-rope walk across Niagara Falls in 1859. A remarkable aspect of The Great Blondin's performance is the multiple crossings he made while carrying various objects, including pushing a wheelbarrow. He would reportedly ask the spectators if they thought he could walk across Niagara Falls blindfolded while pushing the wheelbarrow. The crowd would cheer, "Yes! We think you can!" He would then put on a blindfold and walk across the river while pushing the wheel-barrow. When he reached the other side, he would say to the cheering crowd, "Now I'm going back. Who wants to ride? Are there any volunteers?" No one would dare respond. He would then reiterate his request for a volunteer: "Who wants to ride in the wheelbarrow?" Again, there would be complete silence. Not a single person in the crowd was willing to get into the wheelbarrow; thus, he often had to push it across empty.

Although everyone was convinced that Mr. Gravelet had the skill to safely cross Niagara Falls with the wheelbarrow, no one dared to join him on the journey. According to the crowd's own words, they believed in Mr. Gravelet's ability to cross to the other side; they just did not "believe in" him or his great skills. In other words, they did not trust him with their lives.

This story shows us that there's a big difference between just accepting that someone can do something versus making life and death decisions based on that person's capabilities. That's what Jesus is talking about when He says we have to believe in Him—not just believe *about* Him.

The Lord Jesus guarantees eternal life not to those who believe Him, but to those who truly believe in Him (John 3:16).

* * *

Having shed some light on the meaning of belief in John 3:16, let us return to our original questions concerning the interrelationship between faith, belief, and obedience. An etymological comparison of these words reveals that belief originally meant "trust in God" until the early 13th century, while faith referred to "loyalty to a person based on promise or duty."

Beginning with 14th-century translations, faith took on a religious connotation, whereas belief became limited to "mental acceptance of something as true" by the 16th century[1]; it is no wonder that John 3:16 is often misunderstood today. In modern usage, faith is synonymous with "belief in" as it was in biblical times. The Old Testament gives us accounts of many historical events, and the responses of those who experienced them vividly illustrate what "faith" looks like when manifested in the lives of ordinary people like us.

One of my personal favorites among these accounts is found in Daniel 3, where we see three young Hebrew men responding to a life-and-death situation in a manner that boldly displays their faith in God. Clearly ordered by the king himself that the consequence of their continued refusal to worship the golden image would be a painful death in the fiery furnace, Shadrach, Meshach, and Abed-Nego responded to King Nebuchadnezzar, saying: "O Nebuchadnezzar, we have no need to answer you in this matter. If that is the case, our God whom we serve is able to deliver us from the burning fiery furnace, and He will deliver us from your hand, O king; but if not, let it be known to you, O king, that we do not serve your gods, nor will we worship the gold image which you have set up."

It is unequivocally clear from their words that these men possessed

---

[1] Douglas Harper, Online Etymology Dictionary.

absolute trust in God. They believed that God was mighty to save them if He chose to do so. However, what makes their response remarkable is that they were also prepared to perish while trusting and obeying God, even if, by His supreme and flawless will, He chose not to save them. That is faith in action!

The full account of this event concerning Shadrach, Meshach, and Abed-Nego clearly demonstrates that God is mighty to save, even from a fiery furnace. Better yet, it shows us what *saving faith* looks like in real-life circumstances: total trust in God and obedience to Him and His Christ, despite the consequences. This is the only kind of faith that saves. The Lord Jesus Christ affirmed this in Luke 14:26 when He said to His audience: "If anyone comes to Me and does not hate his father and mother, wife and children, brothers and sisters, yes, and his own life also, he cannot be My disciple. And whoever does not bear his cross and come after Me cannot be My disciple" (NKJV).

Yes, the Christian ought to prioritize obedience to the Lord Jesus Christ above everything else, including his or her own livelihood.

You might ask: what does belief (or faith) have to do with obedience? Well, it has everything to do with it: John the Baptist states in John 3:36 that "anyone who believes in God's Son has eternal life. Anyone who doesn't obey the Son will never experience eternal life but remains under God's angry judgment" (NLT).

Once we know the truth of God's purpose for sending His Son into the world, those who willfully choose to disbelieve do so in rebellion against His holy purpose, which is to save the world through His Son. Believing in the Son equates to obeying Him. Jesus' expectation of obedience from His disciples – Christians – is evident in His frustration with those who claim to be Christians yet deliberately continue to disobey His Word. He highlights the apparent hypocrisy with a question in Luke 6:46 "Why do you call Me 'Lord, Lord,' and not do the things which I say?" (NKJV).

Our discussion of faith in relation to obedience would be incomplete without an account of the significance of obedience in the life of the "Father of Faith," Abraham. In Romans 3:4, the apostle Paul wrote: "Abraham believed God, and it was accounted to him for righteousness" (NKJV). Someone might argue that Paul did not say Abraham believed *in* God; however, a quick look at Genesis 15:6, which is the scripture quoted by Paul in Romans 3:4, dispels any confusion. The passage reads: "And he believed in the Lord, and He accounted it to him for righteousness" (NKJV).

Indeed, Abraham believed in God. He had, in God, the same faith that Jesus says prospective Christians must have in the Savior in order to gain eternal life. Abraham's faith, as obedience in spite of consequences, is best demonstrated through his response to one of the most remarkable events in his journey with God. As recorded in Genesis 22, God said to Abraham:

> Take now your son, your only son Isaac, whom you love,

20

and go to the land of Moriah, and offer him there as a burnt offering on one of the mountains of which I shall tell you.' So, Abraham rose early in the morning and saddled his donkey, and took two of his young men with him... And Abraham stretched out his hand and took the knife to slay his son. But the Angel of the Lord called to him from heaven. (Genesis 22:2-3 and 10-11 NKJV).

Abraham believed in God to the point of wholeheartedly obeying His word, regardless of the consequences for his own life or that of his family. By God's command, he left his father's house, his people, and his country to sojourn in a foreign land, facing a multitude of challenges and life-threatening situations. To test him, God asked for the life of his only son Isaac as a burnt offering; Abraham still obeyed God. That is faith in practice!

There are countless accounts of individuals displaying such faith in God in both the Old and New Testaments. Hebrews 11 states that "all these, having obtained a good testimony through faith, did not receive the promise" (Hebrews 11:39 NKJV). Yet, they remained obedient to God. Granted, most of us will never literally experience the same circumstances as Abraham or Shadrach, Meshach, and Abed-Nego; what is certain is that we routinely face a multitude of less extreme situations where we must make decisions that affect our lives or those of our loved ones in various ways or degrees.

The question is whether we make those decisions with our Christian faith in perspective. For instance, do we still tell the truth even if it means being fired? Do we maintain our integrity if it means paying a hefty fine for our mistakes? Do we love our enemies? Do we remain honest when we realize that everyone around us is cheating or lying to achieve financial success? Are we prioritizing our careers over the godly upbringing of our children? There is no end to this line of questions; they arise each and every day in the course of life. All the Lord requires of us is to prioritize Him and His interests first.

Our faith determines our priorities, and our priorities are evident through obedience to the Word of God. Living every aspect of our daily lives by God's Word is the essence of the life to which Christians are called.

CHAPTER 3

LOVE

The Divine Purpose for Mankind

"For God so loved the world that he gave his one and only Son, that whoever believes in him shall not perish but have eternal life" (John 3:16 NKJV).

The Bible clearly states that God has loved humanity since the day of Adam and Eve in the garden of Eden. In fact, God's primary desire for a loving relationship with humans is definitely the ultimate motivating factor behind the creation of Man.[2] The Lord Jesus Christ powerfully summed up the divine expectation in this God-man relationship, saying:

"You shall love the Lord your God with all your heart, with all your soul, and with all your mind. This is the first and great commandment. And the second is like it: 'You shall love your neighbor as yourself. On these two commandments hang all the Law and the Prophets" (Matthew 22:37-40 NKJV).

---

[2] For consistency with biblical text, the term 'Man' is used throughout the book as short for mankind.

In other words, God desires for every person to love Him with their whole being! That is the depth of love He seeks in the relationship.

Through His sacrificial death on a Roman cross, the Lord Jesus revealed the immense love God has already poured out and continues to pour into His relationship with humanity. Throughout the Bible, love is the principal motivation of God in His relationship with humankind. Grasping the concept of love in its biblical context is therefore essential for developing an accurate understanding and application of the Scriptures to relationships: both with God and with other people.

Unfortunately, love is perhaps the most misunderstood and misapplied biblical concept. This confusion is partly due to the limitations of English as the target language for translations of the more expressive languages used to write the original manuscripts of the Bible. While the English language has only one word for the concept of love, the more expressive Greek language, originally used to write the New Testament has at least four words that convey the meaning of love more accurately in specific contexts. Among these, *agape* is the Greek word that defines the love of God for humanity. The agape kind of love will be the focus of the remaining paragraphs of this chapter.

Agape Love

It is essential for those who desire insight into God's interaction with mankind to understand what agape love is. Many of the seemingly difficult questions about divine interaction with humanity arise from misconceptions of God's agape love. Understanding agape love also helps develop a realistic perspective on the teachings of the Lord Jesus presented throughout the first four books of the New Testament, for example, "Love your enemy" (Matthew 5:44).

Let us start by stating that agape love does not typically exist between good friends or between a man and a woman who feel attracted to each other. This is so, even though it may develop in those types of human relationships. Agape love is a selfless commitment to look out for someone's interests. As such, it is not motivated by any self-interested pursuit. It is freely granted from the heart to the beneficiary without any strings attached and can therefore be given to a totally undeserving individual. It is in that sense that Jesus commands Christians to love their enemies in imitation of God, who makes the rain fall and the sun shine on the fields of both the unrighteous and the righteous.

Agape love is solely motivated by heartfelt kindness and unmerited favor toward the one who is loved. At times, as humans, we may be fooled by someone claiming to have agape love for us, but the all-knowing God, who searches human hearts, cannot be deceived. He can discern without fail true agape love from any counterfeit. Agape cannot be obtained by coercion, bribery, or deception because it must be motivated by heartfelt kindness and unmerited favor toward the beneficiary.

Although God could have created man without the option to feel otherwise toward Him, doing so would have stripped mankind of its humanity: the capacity to truly love from the heart. Without the option of feeling hate toward God, love for Him would be meaningless. It would not be love.

Robots are very predictable and efficient executors of commands, yet we never use any type of love vocabulary to describe a robot's interaction with its operator. Seriously speaking, no one will ever say, "My brand-new car performs every function that I initiate as a driver; it really loves me!" We do not describe our interactions with robots in terms of love because robots do not have the capacity to willfully disobey orders. They are not capable of feeling kindness or favor toward an operator; they cannot love.

God intended humans to be different, so He made them totally free to make independent decisions to love or hate from the heart. Love cannot meaningfully exist without the option of not loving.

CHAPTER 4

Created Free, Predestined to Glory

F ree will vs. predestination is one of the most controversial subjects in Christian circles today. So much so that an examination of the relative teachings and beliefs often reveals sharp, sometimes contradictory, differences among evangelical churches and even believers within the same congregation. Thus, my attempt to shed light on these subjects may be viewed by critics as pretentious, given that I am neither a renowned Bible scholar nor a seminary graduate. I have never attended such an educational institution.

Despite the risk of open criticism or concealed skepticism from the Christian community, I feel compelled to share what I believe to be the truth about predestination and free will. It is my conviction—and the Lord's promise—that the Holy Spirit reveals the truth on any matter to believers who earnestly and prayerfully study the Scriptures in search of God's will (Mark 4:24-25 NKJV).

Having experienced such a revelation, I am motivated by love for my Christian brothers and sisters to share my convictions on this matter as taught in the Holy Scriptures.

In the remainder of this chapter, we will examine biblical texts in search of logical and meaningful insights into the concepts of pre-destination and free will. To set the stage for a fruitful discussion of these concepts, we must first establish an adequate context. Without such a context, we are likely to engage in a purely philosophical ex-ercise that will not be spiritually fruitful. We need a relevant context where the Bible provides background information that logically[3] ex-plains some of the complexities and seemingly contradictory aspects of *predestination* and *free will*. We believe that one such context springs from the divine motivation that led to the creation of man-kind. So, we will investigate it by examining relevant biblical pas-sages. Therefore, we will investigate it by examining relevant bibli-cal passages.

The creation of mankind is particularly intriguing because God did not intend to make just another creature. He wanted to create some-one to whom He would bestow some of His own divine attributes.

In Genesis 1:26 God said, "Let Us make man in Our image, accord-ing to Our likeness" (NKJV). Why did Almighty God desire such a being? What was the divine purpose in the creation of mankind?

---

[3] Some may argue that Christianity is all about belief, not logic. My response to their argument is: Would the creator who gave mankind its capacity to think and act logically be lacking in those qualities? Absolutely not. Faith does not exclude logical reasoning; it merely complements our lack of understand-ing in the things of an infinitely wise creator, enabling us to come to terms with these by simply trusting in God.

Throughout the Bible, it is abundantly clear that God's ultimate purpose for creating mankind was and still is to live in a loving relationship with this special creation of His.

This divine purpose is profoundly significant because it not only defines who mankind was created to be but also explains the relationship that God has been pursuing with humanity since its creation in the garden of Eden. God's purpose in creating mankind sheds light on wonderful and perplexing biblical truths such as free will, sin, salvation, and election (also known as predestination).

In the following paragraphs, we will examine free will, sin, and election in the context of the divine purpose for mankind. We will begin our discussion of each of these concepts with a biblical definition, followed by a discussion of its necessity as an integral part of God's purpose for humanity.

* * *

Free Will: The Freedom to Choose without Divine Interference
What is free will? Can mankind be free in the presence of an almighty and all-knowing Creator? Yes! Spiritual freedom is not the opposite of rules; it is the ability to choose freely without any interference from God. Indeed, if spiritual freedom is granted to mankind by the almighty Creator, including freedom from God, man would truly be free. As we will see, the biblical truth is that God inherently bestowed spiritual freedom upon humanity at creation.

Among all people living in modern times, Americans have a unique perspective and appreciation for freedom as an inalienable right endowed to mankind by the Creator. Indeed, God created us as morally free agents! Yes, we have the capacity to exercise freedom, even freedom from the Creator.

The all-knowing Creator of the universe, the Lord God Almighty, having predetermined the set of possible alternatives, has instilled in us the capacity for free will to make moral choices within that predetermined set of possibilities. He has done so without any inherently biased interference from Him that would sway the choices ultimately made. For every moral decision we face in this life, although the relative circumstances may influence our ultimate choices, we have the inherent capacity to make those choices freely. We can make selfish or selfless decisions; that is, decisions that are either beneficial or detrimental to others, decisions to obey or disobey God, and yes, decisions to love or hate God. From the days of Adam and Eve in the garden of Eden to the present age, humans have been exercising this divine capability bestowed by their Creator. That is *free* will.

.

* * *

Free Will: Essential Quality or Flaw

In light of biblical and historical accounts of mankind's exercise of freedom, free will may be perceived as a negative attribute of humanity. After all, it enabled the original sin. One might argue that without mankind's ability to disobey God's command, there could not have been any possibility of sin entering the world, and that is a valid argument. Some may even go so far as to blame the Creator for making such a flawed creature—a seemingly just accusation. However, such views of free will are fraught with questions that ultimately contradict the attributes of God as conveyed through Scripture. This contradiction alone clearly indicates that the underlying views are biblically incorrect.

Our view of free will is quite the opposite of those mentioned above. Free will is a divine attribute! In John 6:38-40, Jesus says,

> For I have come down from heaven not to do my will but to do the will of him who sent me. And this is the will of him who sent me, that I shall lose none of all that he has given me, but raise them up at the last day. For my Father's will is that everyone who looks to the Son and believes in him shall have eternal life, and I will raise him up at the last day. (NIV)

It is clear from this passage that both the Son and the Father have a will. It is also evident that the Son chose to do the Father's will, not His own. Being endowed with free will is neither sinful nor a temptation to sin. Jesus Christ, the sinless Redeemer of mankind, has a will, which He chose to lay down "to do the will of him who sent" Him. And He did so without committing a single sin.

Free will is a divine attribute bestowed on man, an enabler of the Creator's image in the creature. The misuse of this divine attribute does not tarnish the attribute itself; it only corrupts its possessor: the creature.

The question still remains: why did mankind have to be endowed with free will? The easy—but not so insightful—answer to this question is that God desired it to be so. This answer soon proves too shallow in light of the far-reaching consequences of mankind's historical exercise of free will.

The consequences of the original sin in the garden of Eden are extensive for both the creature and the Creator:

1. The creature was destined for eternal separation and damnation from the Creator.
2. The Creator had to incur a very high cost—the crucifixion of His Son—to redeem the creature.

This raises the question of whether endowing mankind with free will was worth all the trouble, so to speak. The answer to this rhetorical question is emphatically, yes! The Lord God Almighty is omniscient; that is, He is all-knowing. He knows everything, including the details of all past, present, and future events. As a result, none of the occurrences in the garden of Eden came as a surprise to Him. He knew that creating Adam and Eve with the freedom to make choices without divine interference meant they could go against His will if they chose. Still, He did it. We can therefore conclude, with unwavering certainty, that it was worth it! But why was it worth it, you may wonder?

Free Will: The Essence of Mankind

There may be several reasons why the Creator of the universe made man with free will. However, one reason, above all the others, leads to His ultimate purpose for creating man. In Mark 12:30-31, Jesus states the following as the greatest commandment: "Love the Lord your God with all your heart and with all your soul and with all your mind and with all your strength… Love your neighbor as yourself" (NIV).

Even though the Lord's statement is not literally found in the Ten Commandments, it is an all-encompassing and powerful summary of them. From this statement, it is clear that the primary purpose of man is to glorify God by loving Him with all his heart, soul, mind, and strength, and loving his neighbor as himself. "What does loving God and my neighbor have to do with free will?"

To provide a meaningful answer to that question, we must acknowledge some basic facts about the nature of love. Regardless of our individual interpretations of love, we can all agree on one thing: love is unconditionally given; it is a freely offered favor. Obedience is not love; it may be motivated by love, but it is not love itself. An automated response, no matter how reliable and convenient it may be, is certainly not love.

If love is an unconditional, freely given favor, it follows that robots are incapable of loving. That is why no sensible person would ever say, "My robot vacuum continuously cleans my carpet while I am at work; it really loves me!" Only truly free and living beings are capable of loving in a genuine and etymological sense.

I dare say that from the Creator's perspective, the true glory given to Him by such a free and self-motivated creature overshadows the risk that such a creature might reject Him. For this reason, the all-knowing God created mankind with the perfectly fitting capability: free will. In other words, God, in His omniscience, intentionally created Adam with the capacity to freely obey or disobey, love or hate, choose to remain innocent or become sinful. Free will is not a flaw of humanity; it is the fundamental attribute that enables humanity to realize its ultimate divine purpose; it is the essence of what it means to be human. Without it, we cease to be human.

CHAPTER 5

PREDESTINATION
The Divine Redemptive Plan for Mankind

The concept of predestination is first introduced in the New Testament by the Lord Jesus Christ Himself in John 6:37: "All that the Father gives me will come to me, and whoever comes to me I will never drive away" (NIV).

John 6:44 says, "No one can come to me unless the Father who sent me draws him, and I will raise him up at the last day" (NIV).

These verses clearly convey that no one comes to a faith-enabling knowledge of Christ unless God the Father "draws him." But what does the Lord Jesus mean by the Father drawing someone? Do these statements indicate that God the Father actively participates in one's coming to the Savior? Certainly!

Predestination is also taught by the apostle Paul in the following biblical passages:

And we know that in all things God works for the good of those who love him, who have been called according to his purpose. For those God foreknew he also predestined to be conformed to the likeness of his Son, that he might be the firstborn among many brothers. And those he predestined, he also called; those he called, he also justified; those he justified, he also glorified. (Romans 8:28-30 NIV)

Praise be to God the Father of our Lord Jesus Christ, who has blessed us in the heavenly realms with every spiritual blessing in Christ. For he chose us in him before the creation of the world to be holy and blameless in his sight. In love, he predestined us to be adopted as his sons through Jesus Christ, in accordance with his pleasure and will—to the praise of his glorious grace, which he has freely given us in the One he loves. (Ephesians 1:3-6 NIV).

In him we were also chosen, having been predestined according to the plan of him who works out everything in conformity with the purpose of his will, in order that we, who were the first to hope in Christ, might be for the praise of his glory. And you also were included in Christ when you heard the word of truth, the gospel of your salvation. Having believed, you were marked in him with a seal, the promised Holy Spirit, who is a deposit guaranteeing our inheritance until the redemption of those who are God's possession—to the praise of his glory. (Ephesians 1:11-14 NIV)

Do these statements imply that those coming to the Savior have no participation or choice in the matter? It certainly seems so! Does this mean that God the Father draws some people to eternal life in Christ while leaving others to perish in hell? Given the number of lost souls throughout human history, we might be tempted to answer affirmatively. However, the omniscient Savior, knowing how controversial these statements could be if taken alone, provided further explanations. In fact, the Lord Jesus elaborated in John 6:45, where He states: "It is written in the Prophets: 'They will all be taught by God.' Everyone who listens to the Father and learns from him comes to me" (NIV).

The Lord Jesus is simply saying that God the Father is the teacher of all mankind and that "everyone who listens to the Father and learns from him comes to" Him, the Savior. Note the precision in the Lord's words. The Father teaches mankind. The responsibility and free choice of humanity is to heed God's teaching. Will some people freely choose not to listen? Absolutely.

Perhaps the Father is biased in the way He teaches people? Several biblical passages provide insight into the Father's teaching methods; a closer look reveals that the Father teaches humanity in various ways, with His creation (the universe) and His Word (the Bible) being the primary means of instruction.

As King David stated in Psalm 19:1-4, "The heavens declare the glory of God; the skies proclaim the work of his hands. Day after day, they pour forth speech; night after night, they display knowledge. There is no speech or language where their voice is not heard. Their voice goes out into all the earth, their words to the ends of the world" (NIV).

The apostle Paul also echoes this idea of God the Father teaching mankind through creation in Romans 1:20, stating: "For since the creation of the world God's invisible qualities—his eternal power and divine nature—have been clearly seen, being understood from what has been made, so that men are without excuse" (NIV).

The Father's use of His Word as a primary means of teaching humanity is evident throughout the Bible. For example, God taught Israel through His Word in the form of the written law given to Moses, as well as through commands communicated orally by the prophets. Jesus Christ—the Word of God made flesh—is the ultimate means used by the Father to teach mankind.

In Hebrews 1:1-2, the apostle Paul states: "In the past God spoke to our forefathers through the prophets at many times and in various ways, but in these last days he has spoken to us by his Son, whom he appointed heir of all things, and through whom he made the universe" (NIV), confirming the Father's teaching of mankind through Jesus Christ, the Son of God.

The Lord Jesus Himself said in John 7:16-17, "My teaching is not my own. It comes from him who sent me. If anyone chooses to do God's will, he will find out whether my teaching comes from God or whether I speak on my own" (NIV).

He reiterates this in John 14:24, "He who does not love me will not obey my teaching. These words you hear are not my own; they belong to the Father who sent me" (NIV). So, if the primary means by which the Father teaches mankind are His visible creation and written Word, both of which are widely available today, why do some believe and others do not? I contend that the responsibility lies with humanity. Have you ever wondered why the Lord Jesus' last command to His disciples was to go into the world, make disciples, and teach them how to practice what they have been taught? Perhaps this was the most important task He wanted them to carry out after His departure from Earth? I am convinced of its significance, given the tragedies that the Lord knew would befall the disciples in the process.

Would the Lord Jesus have sent His beloved disciples to die horrible deaths for no reason? "Absolutely not!" you might reply. Well, that is what one would imply by a statement suggesting that God the Father decided, before the foundation of the world, who among us He ultimately wants in heaven and who He utterly condemns to hell. There would be no need to go into the world and preach to anyone because the Father would have already sealed the fate of each living human being. We will return to this point regarding the Great Commission in later sections of this chapter.

It is interesting to note that the apostle Paul, who wrote the difficult passage that has stirred up all the controversy on predestination, concurs with the Lord Jesus on this process. He provides a complementary explanation in the following verses found in 2 Thessalonians 2:13-14, "But we ought always to thank God for you, brothers loved by the Lord, because from the beginning God chose you to be saved through the sanctifying work of the Spirit and through belief in the truth. He called you to this through our gospel, that you might share in the glory of our Lord Jesus Christ" (NIV).

The apostle Paul clearly conveys that, from the beginning, God made plans for believers "to be saved through the sanctifying work of the Spirit and through belief in the truth." He explains that it is through the gospel that God calls each one to salvation, so they "might share in the glory of our Lord Jesus Christ." In other words, the gospel is the vehicle that God uses to teach the unbeliever.

The unbeliever's response to the gospel: "belief in the truth," ultimately determines whether he or she benefits from God's pre-established plans: sharing "in the glory of our Lord Jesus Christ," or is condemned to eternal separation from God. Note that the sanctifying work of the Holy Spirit pertains only to the believer and is not a factor in the process by which God the Father draws the unbelieving children of man.

* * *

Having covered several Bible verses related to predestination, we are now equipped to examine the details of the process by which God's pre-established plans are made effective in the lives of men and women. To that end, let us ponder a bit on the explanatory statement of the Lord Jesus Christ in John 6:45. How significant is this statement in relation to the preceding passage of John 6:37-45? In this focal passage, the Lord is indeed explaining the idea of predestination—also known as election—that He introduced in John 6:37-45. An examination of the Lord's statement reveals three crucial aspects of the process of predestination: (1) the role of God the Father in the process, (2) the scope of the process, and (3) the responsibility of man in the process.

1. **The Role of the Father**

   John 6:45 explains the process by which God the Father leads someone to saving faith in the Lord Jesus Christ. In this verse, the Lord Jesus states that His Father draws someone to the Savior by means of a faith-enabling knowledge of Christ imparted through teaching. Indeed, "How, then, can they call on the one they have not believed in? And how can they believe in the one of whom they have not heard? And how can they hear without someone preaching to them?" (Romans 10:14 NIV).

2. **The Scope of the Process**

   Predestination has far-reaching doctrinal implications for one's perception of the justice of God, which has been clouded in the minds of many by the long-standing question of whether God the Father draws some to eternal life in Christ while leaving others to perish in hell. Answering this question affirmatively portrays the infinitely just God the Father as a totally unjust being.

Through Scripture, we know that the Father is a God of justice; in fact, He is so just that He can never leave sin unpunished. So much so that He had to give up His Son to death by crucifixion to satisfy His own infinitely just nature. Note that in doing so, the Father was appeasing none other than Himself; that is how amazingly just He is! Consequently, the long-standing question must be answered in the negative. It must indeed, for the Lord Jesus, speaking of the children of man, echoed the prophet Isaiah, saying, "They will all be taught by God."

A pastor I knew many years ago used to say: "ALL means all; and that is all ALL means." Needless to say, without exception, God the Father teaches all the children of man; in other words, He draws all of mankind. In fact, He teaches and waits for the children of man to respond to His teaching. Second Peter 3:9 states: "The Lord is not slow in keeping his promise, as some understand slowness. He is patient with you, not wanting anyone to perish, but everyone to come to repentance" (NIV).

3. **The Responsibility of Man in the Predestination Process**
   As stated by the Lord Jesus in John 6:45, speaking of unbelievers, "They will all be taught by God. Everyone who listens to the Father and learns from him comes to me" (NIV). It is clear that the unbeliever has a responsibility in the election process; that is, to listen "to the Father and learn from him."

The Lord Jesus indicates that everyone who embraces that responsibility inevitably comes to Him. Let us carefully examine what He meant by listening and learning from the Father. This listening and learning is a response to the Father's teaching; it involves a moral obligation to act on God's instruction by accepting His plan of salvation for mankind. One might argue that the ability to listen to the Father and learn from Him is granted by the Father only to the elect. Such an argument is fundamentally flawed in light of Romans 1:20, where the apostle Paul states that the eternal power and divine nature of God have been evident from the beginning, "Being understood from what has been made, so that men are without excuse."

This argument also contradicts 2 Peter 3:9, where the apostle Peter says: "The Lord is not slow in keeping his promise, as some understand slowness. He is patient with you, not wanting anyone to perish, but everyone to come to repentance" (NIV). Did Peter mean everyone who has been chosen beforehand? No, Peter's statement is clear: The Lord desires everyone to come to repentance and be saved.

A Heretic View of Predestination
The question of predestination vs. free will is perhaps one of the most difficult biblical subject matters of all time. However, our lack of understanding of the subject should not lead us to accept propositions that are in clear contradiction with and confuse several fundamental and well-understood biblical teachings.

A view of predestination as a concrete selection of individuals, rather than the institution of selection criteria along with pertinent plans, is one such proposition. The problem with that view is that it leads to the necessary conclusion that almighty God, the judge of the whole earth, unjustly doomed some individuals to hell, and they will not escape their destiny, no matter what kind of life they live on Earth.

Worse, such a proposition strips away our fundamental understanding of several, if not most, Scriptures. Let us consider a few of those scriptures in the following paragraphs.

In John 3:16-18, Jesus said,

> For God so loved the world that he gave his one and only Son, that whoever believes in him shall not perish but have eternal life. For God did not send his Son into the world to condemn the world, but to save the world through him. Whoever believes in him is not condemned, but whoever does not believe stands condemned already because he has not believed in the name of God's one and only Son. (NIV)

Regardless of what the Lord meant by "belief" in this passage, He clearly is saying that the plan of salvation by faith in Himself is extended to everyone, not just some individuals. The argument could be made that saving faith is a gift from God; yes, it is, in the sense that God is the Creator. God created mankind with the capacity of faith. It takes very little thought to realize that we all have faith. God

made us with the ability to freely make an unconditional commitment to love Him and walk with Him.

Man's problem is not that he is incapable of faith; the problem is
that his faith is in someone or something other than the Creator. In
John 3:16-18, the Lord Jesus Christ issues an indictment for whoever misplaces his faith. Is He being disingenuous, blaming the creatures for not doing right, knowing well they have been created without the capacity to do right? God forbid. Man has a responsibility
to take God up on His plan of salvation; that is, to respond to the
gospel with an unwavering commitment to Jesus Christ.

* * *

In addition, a view of predestination as a concrete selection of individuals also obliterates our understanding of the Great Commission.
Before ascending to heaven, the Lord Jesus said to his disciples:

> All authority in heaven and on earth has been given to me.
> Therefore go and make disciples of all nations, baptizing
> them in the name of the Father and of the Son and of the
> Holy Spirit, and teaching them to obey everything I have
> commanded you. And surely, I am with you always, to the
> very end of the age.' (Matthew 28:18-20 NIV)

Since then, there has been tremendous effort and resources committed to fulfilling this command of the Lord. Did He send His disciples
as "sheep among wolves" for a cause without consequence, since

those condemned from the beginning would go to hell, regardless of the apostles' obedience to His command? Absolutely not!

The words of the Apostle Paul in 2 Thessalonians 2:13-14 tell us that the gospel is the channel through which God calls each one to salvation, so that they "might share in the glory of our Lord Jesus Christ." In other words, the gospel is the vehicle that God uses to teach the unbeliever. The unbeliever's response to the gospel, which is "belief in the truth," ultimately determines whether he or she benefits from God's pre-established plans, that of sharing "in the glory of our Lord Jesus Christ."

On the one hand, a positive response grants the unbeliever the privilege of partaking in the eternal glory of the Lord Jesus Christ, i.e., eternal life. On the other hand, a negative response to the gospel, which is a refusal to believe in the truth, condemns the unbeliever to hell, that is, eternal separation from God.

A Biblically Fitting View of Predestination
As used in biblical text, predestination refers to the infinite wisdom of God, the omniscient Creator, in establishing the criteria for eternal life in His kingdom and making plans for those of Adam's race who freely choose to commit unwaveringly to life in His Son, Jesus Christ. "In English, please!" some might say. The following analogy should help clarify what I mean.

Let us imagine that the Department of Public Health of a hypothetical state, eager to mitigate a deadly epidemic, decides to champion free medical treatment for all its residents. The state offers all health services free of charge to each patient, with the sole qualifying criterion being the patient's agreement to receive the needed treatment. Some people, desiring protection from diseases, accept the state's offer despite the temporary, minor side effects fully disclosed by the Department of Public Health. Those residents reap the promised health benefits of the administered therapies. Others, judging the benefits of the therapies not worth the side effects, choose to decline the state's offer and, as a result, do not submit to any of the offered therapies despite the imminent threat of death from the disease.

Can we say that the Department of Public Health predestined the residents to enjoy the benefits that the state offered free of charge? Yes. Are all residents of the state capable and free to accept the state's offer? Yes. Does each resident have a responsibility to make his or her choice for a healthy life effective by accepting the state's offer? Yes. The same applies to the elect concerning God's offer of salvation.

Still, some may ask: How can a loving God allow anyone to go to hell? Isn't the very idea of God allowing such a horrible destiny for some, regardless of their choices, contradictory to the essence of a God who proclaims to be love? These are fair questions that most prospective Christians ask sooner or later. They may not voice these concerns depending on the ethos of the church they attend, but that does not diminish the importance of these questions for the foundation of their faith. It is therefore crucial that even professing Christians be lovingly allowed to ask these questions without being looked down upon. We will discuss these in the rest of this chapter.

Let me start by stating the conclusion of my own past struggle with these age-old questions: God does not send anyone to hell. If you vehemently disagree with my conclusion, you may have legitimate reasons that I will never know or understand. I encourage you to read on and let us examine, in light of the essence of humanity, the reasoning leading to my stated conclusion.

We should recall that God created humans totally free to choose, among other matters, eternal life or death. Eternal life is perpetual existence in harmony and fellowship with God. In contrast, death is a perpetual existence apart from God.

Each of these choices comes with great consequences, both good and bad. The biblical Word of God teaches that, in addition to spending eternity with Him, God promises eternal liberation from the human condition and all its accompanying pains and sufferings.

The Bible also demonstrates that God has been warning humanity about the dire consequences of choosing death since the days of Adam and Eve in the garden of Eden. One could argue that it would be unfair for us to blame God for our choice of death rather than life; however, the premise of our blame goes much deeper: why did the all-knowing God of *love* even make the choice of death possible for humanity?

Why did He create humanity with the propensity to choose death? Could He not have done otherwise? Sure, He could have! The follow-up question, however, is: had God created humanity differently, would humans still be human? Would we, as humans, still meet the divinely set requirements that motivated the creation of humanity in the first place? Would humans still have been capable of truly loving? Does the beauty and benevolence of love carry all its significance without the possibility of hatred? To attempt to answer these questions, let us examine the concept of freedom in a biblical context.

Americans view freedom as an inalienable right; there is biblical wisdom in that perspective. Indeed, freedom *is* an inalienable right: it is a necessary precondition for what it means to be fully human. Without freedom, humans can't fulfill their essential and divinely preset nature and purpose, which are to be capable of truly loving and to live in a loving relationship with God. As we have argued in the previous chapters of this book, true love is and can only be a gift, given from the heart and in total freedom, to another. In that sense, coerced compliance—whether by force or necessity—is not love in a biblical sense.

We can intuitively understand this inherent coupling of freedom and love by considering our relationships, if we can characterize them as such, with familiar and compliant things that we own. Consider the time when you owned a brand-new car; it started and ran flawlessly every time you decided to drive it, regardless of your destination. It stopped when you instructed it to stop by applying the brakes; it accelerated when you pressed on the gas pedal. If you owned such a car in recent years and had automatic climate control, the air conditioner came on when it started to get too hot and stopped when it started to get too cold, etc.

We have only scratched the surface of what a car can automatically do for its driver and passengers these days. Yet, despite all their useful, sometimes life-saving services, we normally do not sincerely claim that we have loving relationships with them. We would not make such claims because we know that cars are machines, in other words, automatons. A perfectly functional car can never decide to disobey its operator and perform the opposite of the function(s) that a received command was designed to execute. Thus, functional robots are very compliant; they are not loving, nor are they capable of love.

In light of the inherent nature of freedom as an essential and defining factor of true love, the compelling answer to the question of whether love can have true meaning without freedom is a resounding "NO!" So, could God have created robots instead of humans? Yes, God is almighty and can do anything He desires to fulfill His divine purposes, including granting total freedom of choice to humanity. What God cannot do is undermine His own determined purpose. Forcing humans to comply with His will does just that.

CHAPTER 6

SIN

Mankind's Misguided Exercise of Free Will

Sin is one of the subject matters most discussed in the Bible. It is referenced more than 957 times, in various ways: at least 808 times in the Old Testament and 146 times in the New Testament. For those who desire insight into relevant matters while making life-changing decisions, understanding the Bible's notion of sin would be a critical aspect of the process of conversion to Christianity, and it would be so for good reasons. For example, it only takes a read through the books of Genesis and John to come to the conclusion that without the existence of sin, there would be no need for salvation and much of the suffering humanity endures.

This begs the following questions: by creating humans with the propensity to sin, did the all-knowing, almighty, perfect God make a mistake? Did He not know what would happen to His creation should mankind sin? In fact, God placed the very thing that aided the culmination of sin in mankind—*"the tree of knowledge of good and evil"* (Genesis 2:9 NKJV)—in "Adam's backyard," the garden of Eden. These are legitimate questions that deserve reasonable an-swers. So, our purpose for this chapter is to provide an exposé of sin from a biblical perspective while attempting to logically answer such questions as may possibly be raised in the inquisitive mind. Let us start with the most basic of such questions: what is sin?

The biblical text mostly refers to sinful matters with words such as transgression(s), trespass(es), iniquity, sin, or sins to convey differ-ent aspects of the subject matter of sin. Transgression is used to ex-press a heart attitude that consists of a spiritual revolt or rebellion against God, regardless of resulting actions from the transgressor. Trespass characterizes a treachery, falsehood, violation, offense, or guiltiness as relating to actions rooted in a transgressive heart. Sins, the plural form of sin, is often used to convey a combination of both transgressions and trespasses. Iniquity is used to convey perversity, moral depravity, evil, or crookedness concretely realized in multi-tudes of trespasses.

Sin, the singular form of the word, is mostly used — especially in the New Testament — to refer to an offense or convey a state of (habitual) sinfulness. The Bible's definition of sin may be summed up as the state of bearing blame or guilt before God.

Origin and Necessary Inherency of Sin
Humanity has blamed the Creator for the existence of sin and all its disastrous effects from the beginning. In Genesis 2:16-17, the Lord God commanded Adam—the first human ever created—saying, "You are free to eat from any tree in the garden; but you must not

eat from the tree of the knowledge of good and evil, for when you eat of it you will surely die" (NIV).

It was a clear and stern warning to protect him from the ultimately disastrous consequences of sin. Yet, after disobeying God's command, when Adam was questioned about whether he had eaten from the tree of the knowledge of good and evil, he answered: "The woman you put here with me—she gave me some fruit from the tree, and I ate it" (Genesis 3:12 NIV). He totally placed the blame on God for putting the woman in the garden with him. From Adam's time to this day, humanity has not ceased to blame God for its sinful deeds and the resulting consequences.

Most people, including Christians, tend to ask accusatory questions such as "How can a loving God allow so much suffering in the world? How can a just God allow such bad things to happen to good people?" The real question behind these is, "How can a just, loving, all-knowing, and almighty God blame man for sin after creating him with the propensity to sin?"

Unless answers that reasonably justify this state of affairs can be found, these questions can undermine the foundation of one's faith in God to the point of casting doubt on the entire existence of a Creator. Unfortunately, these critical questions are often considered heretical in some Christian circles. The truth is that ignoring them leaves even the mature Christian in a state of spiritual bondage. The need for adequate answers is even more critical for the emerging faith of prospective and new believers in their quest for answers.

Who Is to Blame?

We cannot logically answer this question without a deeper under-standing of why sin had to be part of the equation in the creation of man. From the earlier chapters of this book, we recall that humans have been created as total "free agents" to live in a loving relation-ship with God. We also explained that the agape kind of love re-quired between humans and God cannot be obtained through coer-cion, bribery, or deception because it is motivated by heartfelt kind-ness and unjustified favor toward the beneficiary.

Although God could have created man without the option to feel otherwise toward Him, doing so would have stripped mankind of its humanity: the capacity to truly love from the heart. Without the op-tion of feeling hate toward God, love for Him would be innate con-ditioning; it would not be love at all. Mankind's capacity to love or not love inherently results from free will, which is the essence of being human. By design, it is impossible for humans to genuinely love and, at the same time, be incapable of choosing to do otherwise. The fact that humans can choose to disobey God is not the result of an unforeseen design flaw for which blame should be laid on God. It is an inherent and essential characteristic of humanity: we cease to be humans without our capacity to freely choose. Therefore, we cannot rightfully blame God for man's capacity to sin. With it, hu-mans were created with full power and independent capacity to choose sin or righteousness.

Practice of Sin

Sin is any act or decision—or lack thereof—that one undertakes against the will of God. As such, there are sins of commission and sins of omission. Sins of the former kind are acts committed or decisions made in disobedience to God's will, as expressed in His Word or naturally revealed through the wonders of the universe, His creation. Sins of the latter kind include failing to take righteous action or make decisions when one is aware of circumstances that call for them. You may think that intentionally avoiding awareness can shield a person from sins of omission, but there is a catch: the very decision to avoid knowing about a situation in order to evade acting or making related decisions is a sin of commission; there are no loopholes!

From a secular and cultural point of view, an act is considered bad only when it results in some type of loss for a person, society, the environment, and so forth. God's standard goes far beyond actions to encompass the very decisions to act, regardless of the opportunity—or lack thereof—to concretely take such actions. This is the biblical principle that the Lord Jesus taught in Matthew Chapter 5.

Note that mere thoughts are not sinful until a decision is made to entertain or act on them. We should also recognize that actions alone, without intent, are not always sinful. The intent motivating the action is paramount as far as God is concerned. Were that not the case, married male gynecologists would be committing adultery several times a day, every business day of the week. In contrast, the decision to interact with or fantasize about someone other than one's spouse is considered sexual immorality in God's eyes, provided that the decision is made to satisfy a sexual desire.

Appreciating the beauty of a lady does not become sinful until one begins to entertain lustful thoughts beyond mere appreciation. Similarly, deciding to kill someone is considered murder in God's eyes, whether the act physically occurs or not. Ultimately, it all returns to the decision to act; whether the action is physically taken or not is irrelevant. Being angry with someone does not become sinful until a decision is made to hurt that person in some way. Watching someone unjustly suffer does not become sinful until one decides to turn a blind eye to the situation and ignore it.

Effects of Sin

The evident effects of sin are all around us; if you disagree, just watch the news reports on your television for a few minutes, and you will soon be convinced. Thus, we will not discuss those further in this book. Instead, we will focus our analysis on the subtleties of biblical passages that address the effects of sin. We shall begin our analysis in Genesis 1:27, which states: "So God created mankind in his own image, in the image of God he created them; male and female he created them" (NIV).

Genesis 5:1-2 reiterates: "When God created mankind, he made them in the likeness of God. He created them male and female and blessed them. And he named them 'Mankind' when they were created" (NIV).

The key term for us to understand in these passages is "image" (also known as likeness). It "does not consist in bodily form; it can only reside in spiritual qualities, in man's mental and moral attributes as a self-conscious, rational, personal agent, capable of self-determination and obedience to moral law."[4]

The referenced biblical passages clearly state that Adam and Eve were created in God's own image. In contrast, "When Adam had lived 130 years, he had a son in his own likeness, in his own image; and he named him Seth" (Genesis 5:3 NIV). Note the difference between Adam, Eve, and their son Seth, in terms of whose image they bore; Adam and Eve were created in God's own image, but they had Seth in Adam's image. What is the difference? A casual reading of these passages might suggest that they are stating the same thing because Seth, as a human, also bore the image of God. That is partly true, but not entirely accurate.

Why didn't the scripture simply say that "Adam had a son also in God's image"? Doing so would have been inaccurate because Adam's image, at the time of his son's birth, no longer accurately reflected God: sin had already tainted and distorted the original image of God that Adam and Eve received at creation (see Genesis 2). Hence, Genesis 5:3 is very precise as stated. What can we conclude from this observation? The effects of the parents' sin extend far beyond the sinner himself and in ways that we might underestimate. They introduce deeper corruption into the sinner's whole being—morally, psychologically, emotionally, spiritually, and sometimes physically.

---

[4] Orr, James, M.A., D.D. General Editor. "Entry for 'GOD, IMAGE OF'". "International Standard Bible Encyclopedia". 1915.

It is interesting to realize that preliminary secular research results[5] are leaning toward this conclusion. So, every sin committed by a father degrades the corrupted image of God that he received from his parents at birth. That father then passes a slightly more corrupted image to his children. The children further corrupt what remains of God's image received from their parents, degrading it even more with their own sins. Thus, the progressive degeneration of the original image of God given to humanity at creation continues.

In some Christian circles, the enduring effects of sin reverberating through generations are referred to as "generational curses." The truth is that the cumulative effect of sins committed by parents increases the predisposition of their descendants to repeat the same sins and more. For instance, the descendants of abused children are more likely to become abusive themselves. It is no wonder that from the day of Adam's sin to the present, sin has been perpetuated throughout the generations of mankind.

The good news is that this human condition is not hopeless: the descendants of sinners are not destined to automatically repeat their parents' sins or burden themselves and their own children without any choice. The free will of each descendant still exists, enabling individuals to make better choices and avoid repeating their parents'

---

[5] Nagy A. Youssef et al., The effects of Trauma, with or without PTSD, on Transgenerational DNA Methylation Alterations in Human Offsprings, Brain Sciences, May 2018; 8(5): 83.

sins—consider the example of Josiah, the ninth king of the Northern Kingdom of Israel (2 Kings 21–22).

Sin has caused pain and suffering for humanity since the days of Adam, but what is its ultimate stark effect? Romans 6:23 states that "The wages of sin is death, but the gift of God is eternal life in Christ Jesus our Lord" (NIV). From this, we understand that those who have received God's gift of eternal life through faith in Christ Jesus are saved from the ultimate effect of sin, which is eternal separation from God and continual torment in hell. Does this mean that believers are immune to the effects of sin? In other words, do believers possess a "get out of jail free" card regarding the effects of sin?

In light of what the Bible teaches us about the redemptive sacrifice of the Lord Jesus Christ on the cross, we know that believers are saved from hell. Nevertheless, they still experience the agony that the burden of sin imposes on all of creation. The consequences of humanity's sins affect both believers and unbelievers; it is clear that believers are not shielded from the natural effects of sin. However, there are controversies surrounding the sins of believers. Can believers sin without consequences? Absolutely not! The same God who extends His infinite grace to sinners is also infinitely just. In fact, He is so just that, for the sake of His own justice, He could not forgo the sacrifice of His only begotten Son on a Roman cross.

Let's consider this for a moment. God is almighty and supreme; He does not have to answer to any being but Himself. Therefore, He could have simply forgiven humanity's sin and spared His Son the agony of the cross; or could He? I would argue that His infinitely just nature would not tolerate sweeping humanity's sin under the rug! There had to be payment for the wrong done in order for God's infinitely perfect justice to be served.

What God did on the cross with His only Son, Jesus Christ, was solely to appease His own wrath and satisfy the impartiality of His own justice! It is, therefore, delusional to think that a self-proclaimed believer can continue to sin casually and escape consequences.

The repented sins of believers will not condemn them to hell. Christ paid for those on the cross—but the Lord still chastens and corrects His rebellious children, even to the point of physical death (1 Corinthians 11:30).

God's Remedy for Sin

Man is guilty and hopelessly condemned to eternal damnation, but thanks be to the **omniscient** God who, knowing the destiny of His beloved creation, made plans to redeem it. The biblical term for the total sum of these plans is "salvation"! Thus, salvation is not an afterthought; it is an original plan divinely crafted from the beginning. It was and still is God's intention to address the ultimate effect of sin on humanity. Indeed, through belief in Jesus Christ and the price paid by His blood shed on the cross, God provided a way for each person to be acquitted from the just punishment for sin—eternal suffering in hell, away from God.

The plan, divinely established from the beginning to save those who believe in the Son of God, is what Paul refers to as predestination! It is not a biased plan devised for some people to share the glory of Christ in heaven while condemning others to hell even before their existence. What kind of just God would do such a thing? Definitely not the God of Abraham. Recall that He was willing to spare the entire cities of Sodom and Gomorrah if He could find even ten right-eous people there (Genesis 18:23-32). We shall take a closer look at how God's plan of salvation is executed in the next chapter.

CHAPTER 7

SALVATION
Restoring Mankind's Lost Divine Image

From the Old to the New Testament, the Bible repeatedly makes references to God's saving grace, or salvation. In this chapter, we will take a closer look at that term under the biblical microscope, so to speak. What is salvation? Do all references to salvation carry the same meaning throughout the Bible? Not likely. Salvation is sometimes used to refer to a gift already given; at other times, it denotes a promise. Are the different meanings of salvation related? If so, how? Is salvation free? How do we receive the gift and promise of salvation?

Salvation Is Not Free; It Is Priceless!

As used in a biblical context, salvation refers to the process that God has established to save each person who believes in Jesus Christ. It is important to note that salvation is a process; contrary to popular teachings disseminated in many churches today, it is not an event that occurs at a specific moment in a believer's life. It is a three-phased process with past, present, and future stages for all who believe. When Brother John Doe says, "I was saved Saturday, December 31, 2016," he is really saying that he began to believe in Jesus Christ and professed Him as Lord and Savior for the first time on that day. These phases of salvation are clearly outlined in the Scriptures, and Bible scholars refer to them as justification, sanctification, and glorification.

In this chapter, we will examine these phases through a study of pertinent scriptures. Additionally, we will explore the perspective of salvation as a free gift. Furthermore, we will address the question of whether a believer's salvation can be lost.

* * *

Justification: Paying for the Penalty of Mankind's Sin

A man found guilty of a capital offense stands in court to be sentenced to death. To his amazement, he hears the judge announce that another man, unknown to the convict, has requested and been granted the right to bear the sentence in place of the convict, with the stipulation that the convict be totally discharged of all wrongdoing, provided he agrees to the deal. The convict accepts the unknown man's offer and is declared blameless and a free man.

From God's perspective, every descendant of Adam is like that convicted criminal, and Jesus Christ is analogous to the unknown man who gave his own life to justify that of the convict. Judicially, justification is the action of showing something to be right or reasonable.

64

From a biblical perspective, justification refers to the right standing before God of one who believes in His Son, Jesus Christ. It is the first stage of God's plan to redeem mankind. He grants it freely to whoever believes in Jesus Christ, regardless of the severity of past sins.

Whoever believes that Jesus Christ died, shedding His precious blood for the remission of sins, is declared legally righteous by God, the merciful judge of the world. Note that nothing other than God's unceasing love, grace, and mercy for mankind moved Him to offer justification to believers; for "There is none righteous, no, not one; There is none who understands; There is none who seeks after God. They have all turned aside; They have together become unprofitable; There is none who does good, no, not one" (Romans 3:10-12 NKJV).

Additionally, the Lord Jesus Christ states in John 3:16 that it is God's love for the world that prompted Him to give His Son for the salvation of those who believe.

In Romans 3:23-25, the apostle Paul writes:

> For everyone has sinned; we all fall short of God's glorious standard. Yet God, with undeserved kindness, declares that we are righteous. He did this through Christ Jesus when he freed us from the penalty for our sins. For God presented Jesus as the sacrifice for sin. People are made right with God when they believe that Jesus sacrificed his life, shedding his blood. (NLT)

It is clear that mankind has no involvement in the origin of justification. With little thought on the matter, we come to understand that the Lord God Almighty, the owner of the universe, which includes mankind, has no need that He cannot fulfill on His own without our help. Even if it were not so, the price of justification—that is, the death of God's Son on a Roman cross—is so high that no human could ever pay for it. No human has anything of sufficient value to exchange for the blood of God's Son. Were God to require an equitable trade for justification, no one could be justified. Thus, God offers justification based on faith in the sacrifice of His Son. It is free and priceless. Still, the question remains: does the fact that mankind has no involvement in bringing about justification make salvation free?

* * *

Sanctification: Retraining Mankind to Embrace Spiritual Life
The New Testament makes it clear that no one is saved apart from faith in Christ Jesus. We also understand that faith in Jesus Christ entails acceptance of Him as Lord and Savior, that is, commitment and obedience to Him and His prescribed way of life.

The Lord Jesus Himself said that there is a cost to following Him (Luke 14:28-33); anyone who has ever lived the Christian life couldn't agree more. Does this mean that we obtain salvation in exchange for our faith in Christ and its implied cost? No, absolutely not! As we have discussed in the previous paragraphs, justification is the first stage of salvation, and it is priceless. Therefore, no claim can be legitimately made about Christian salvation. Nevertheless, salvation encompasses the stage of sanctification, a process that requires human involvement, with requirements that are in constant conflict with man's fallen nature.

Sanctification is the process designed by God to restore and enable the believer to fulfill the primary purpose of the Creator. It is not a price to pay to be saved, albeit from a human perspective, sanctification demands life-changing choices and sacrifices that are totally unnatural. Let us review some of these in the words of the Lord Jesus.

In Luke 14:28-33, He says:

> If you want to be my disciple, you must hate everyone else by comparison—your father and mother, wife and children, brothers and sisters—yes, even your own life. Otherwise, you cannot be my disciple. And if you do not carry your own cross and follow me, you cannot be my disciple. But don't begin until you count the cost. For who would begin construction of a building without first calculating the cost to see if there is enough money to finish it? Otherwise, you might complete only the foundation before running out of money, and then everyone would laugh at you. They would say, 'There's the person who started that building and couldn't afford to finish it!'

Or what king would go to war against another king without first sitting down with his counselors to discuss whether his army of 10,000 could defeat the 20,000 soldiers marching against him? And if he can't, he will send a delegation to discuss terms of peace while the enemy is still far away. So you cannot become my disciple without giving up everything you own. (NLT)

In the Sermon on the Mount, Jesus also said, in Matthew 5:21-22, 27-28, 38-44:

You have heard that it was said to those of old, 'You shall not murder, and whoever murders will be in danger of the judgment.' But I say to you that whoever is angry with his brother without a cause shall be in danger of the judgment. And whoever says to his brother, 'Raca!' shall be in danger of the council. But whoever says, 'You fool!' shall be in danger of hell fire... You have heard that it was said to those of old, 'You shall not commit adultery.' But I say to you that whoever looks at a woman to lust for her has already committed adultery with her in his heart... You have heard that it was said, 'An eye for an eye and a tooth for a tooth.' But I tell you not to resist an evil person. But whoever slaps you on your right cheek, turn the other to him also. If anyone wants to sue you and take away your tunic, let him have your cloak also. And whoever compels you to go one mile, go with him two. Give to him who asks you, and from him who wants to borrow from you do not turn away. You have heard that it was said, 'You shall love your neighbor and hate your enemy.' But I say to you, love your enemies, bless those who curse you, do good to those who hate you, and pray for those who spitefully use you and persecute you. (KJV)

Sanctification clearly entails a supreme love for Jesus, evidenced by life-changing choices on the believer's part; thus, our perception of its cost. In Romans 12:1, the apostle Paul describes it as offering one's being as a living sacrifice. Nevertheless, the apparent cost of sanctification is only perceived as such by mankind. To God, sanctification is a process designed only to restore and enable the believer to fulfill the primary purpose of the Creator. It is not a price to pay to be saved; the thief who believed in Christ while they were both nailed to die on crosses would still be going to hell otherwise. Yet, Jesus promised to be with him in paradise on the very day of their crucifixion (Luke 23:43).

What then? Is sanctification an optional stage of salvation? Not for everyone! This sounds outrageously unfair in light of the egregious sufferings and deaths that so many Christians have undergone throughout history and are still going through in the name of Christ. From God's perspective, it is not unfair.

The Lord Jesus clearly explains that perspective in the parable of the landowner and the hired workers in Matthew 20:1-15. The point of the parable is that the Lord deals with humans individually; what He offered us, and we accepted is what He promises to honor, and He does not do so in comparison with His dealings with others. So, sanctification is a required stage of salvation for the living believer, just as a full workday was required for the workers hired early in the morning to receive their agreed-upon wages.

Believers on this side of eternity must be committed to obeying the words of Jesus. A lack of commitment to Christ and His Word only reveals a lack of faith in Him.

The above-quoted words of Jesus illustrate, in practical terms, how believers ought to love God and their neighbors: "'You shall love the Lord your God with all your heart, with all your soul, with all your strength, and with all your mind,' and 'your neighbor as yourself'" (Luke 10:27 NKJV). So, as long as we are alive in this life, we must undergo sanctification; the Lord Jesus commands it.

Sanctification is humanly impossible. Thank God for the Holy Spirit who, by His regenerative power, continuously works to sanctify the believer through the cleansing of God's Word and the renewing of the believer's mind.

I knew a man who lived in an African village some time ago. He was born in a heathen society where the worship of spirits and the practice of witchcraft were prevalent, especially for him as a village chief's son. In fact, the man was named after a powerful legion of spirits that his family had been worshiping for generations before he was born.

He was taught from childhood that the spirits after which he was named were the protectors of his family at large. In exchange for their protection, the spirits' mandates for the man's family and their descendants were to strictly refrain from going to their farms on Fridays, eating meals cooked by a woman during her menstrual cycle, and eating any meat from all birds of the air as well as all farmed animals, including chicken, beef, lamb, goat, etc. The only flying animals that were not off-limits for them were the yellow African bats.

The penalty for failing to obey those rules was death inflicted by the spirits on family members unless they were acceptably appeased through sacrificial offerings.

From his youth, the man strictly observed those mandates in addition to the prescribed offerings that he had to regularly provide to appease the spirits. As a young man, he married and started a family with his wife. He also began to assume his leadership roles as a trained practitioner of the secret rituals of his society. He was a leader of the public dance club of the village and, as such, regularly organized and attended parties with his friends. He was well-versed and an active participant in the secret dances and associated rituals. He also had a few girlfriends in addition to several other young ladies who openly rivaled his wife and expressed interest in him, the chief's son.

Needless to say, the man did not know God in his youth. He was a member of a large family that counted a dozen men and fourteen women living in a large compound founded by his father, the village chief. By many traditional African societal criteria, he was privileged and successful; yet, the man was dying inside. He was losing his children to sudden and mysterious deaths between the ages of one and seven years. With each loss came the obligation to provide a ram, a male goat, and a few hens to perform the sacrifices necessary to appease the spirits.

The man was not just losing his children; he was also spending all he had in the process. He consulted every medium he could find; he offered every sacrifice he was urged to offer; he observed every rule he was prescribed; yet, his children were still dying. He experienced such tragedies successively over a period of ten years, losing a total of four children.

Spending sleepless nights thinking about his family tragedy, he grew more and more desperate for a solution. Frustrated and distressed, the man made his decision to follow Christ one Sunday morning. He got up early and went to the CMA church, newly started in the village, without revealing his intentions to anyone, not even to his wife. He converted to Christianity that day. Upon returning home from the church, he informed his wife about the commitment he had just made to follow Christ. The following Sunday, she accompanied him to the church and converted to Christianity as well. Thus, they started their walk with the Lord and never looked back.

The man abandoned his heritage of spirit worship in spite of the threats and ostracization he faced from the rest of his family. He left his former lifestyle of parties and women to dedicate himself to his wife and serve the Lord to the best of his knowledge. He stopped drinking and left the dance club he once led. He later left his cocoa farm to dedicate his time to the CMA church of the village when he was appointed to lead it, prioritizing service to the Lord over the opportunity to build an earthly treasure for himself and his descendants. He was not a rich man and was denied access to all the inheritance from his father. So, the decision to leave his farm to focus on the needs of the church he was appointed to lead cost him and his immediate family dearly.

He hardly had enough to care for his family and cover his children's school expenses, but he remained faithful to the Lord in spite of the hardship that resulted from his decision to follow Christ. He did not see great tangible blessings from the Lord, but his children abundantly did.

He was a man of few words who viewed any personal attacks against him as a deceptive trick from the Devil to derail him from his walk with the Lord, and he quickly dissipated any conflict with gracious responses to such attacks. He was a peaceful and generous man who endured abuse from his detractors without retaliation. He was never caught bad-mouthing anyone, not even his enemies; if he heard anyone in his family criticizing someone, he swiftly put an end to such conversations, saying, "Please stop criticizing people. If you have copied that manner of speech from me, I urge you to stop."

He was a man of integrity who taught his children to walk in the same way. His last words to his son were: "Serve the Lord whole-heartedly, pursue your career with integrity, and do not deal treacherously with anyone in business or any other domain of life; and may the Lord bless you."

The man never attended school, but he learned to read in order to study the Scriptures. He regularly studied them, and the more he learned from them, the more he practiced the biblical principles in his daily life. The more he practiced those principles, the more apparent their impact on his life was for all to see. A testimony from his wife confirmed the progressive and apparent transformation of the man's worldview and character throughout his life. Certainly, that man was not sinless—no one but Jesus Christ has ever been or will ever be on earth—but the renewing of his mind, the progressive Christlike transformation of his worldview, character, and way of life all testify to his sanctification as a Christian.

The books of Matthew, Mark, Luke, and John also provide several examples of Christians who went through the sanctification process; the list includes Mary of Magdala—aka Mary Magdalene—who went from prostitution to believer and loyal follower of Christ, Zacchaeus the tax collector (Luke 19:8–10), Matthew the tax collector who became an apostle of Christ, and the apostle Paul. Even one of the criminals crucified along with Christ, who came to believe in Him in the last moments of his life, started his sanctification process before his death (Luke 23:39-43).

Glorification: Restoring Mankind to its Originally Given Divine Nature

Glorification is the final step and ultimate goal of salvation. It consists of the elevation of believers to the nature and being of Christ, which will occur when He returns to Earth to gather those who believe in Him.

The Bible teaches that glorified believers will be known as they are, but their bodies will be transformed into the likeness of Christ's resurrected body. First Corinthians 15:50-54 provides a glimpse of what such a body will be:

> I declare to you, brothers and sisters, that flesh and blood cannot inherit the kingdom of God, nor does the perishable inherit the imperishable. Listen, I tell you a mystery: We will not all sleep, but we will all be changed—in a flash, in the twinkling of an eye, at the last trumpet. For the trumpet will sound, the dead will be raised imperishable, and we will be changed. For the perishable must clothe itself with the imperishable, and the mortal with immortality. When the perishable has been clothed with the imperishable, and the mortal with immortality, then the saying that is written will come true: 'Death has been swallowed up in victory.' (NIV)

From this passage, we know that the dead will be raised to life from the grave and clothed in imperishable and immortal bodies like Christ's. The living will not die, but their bodies will also be instantly transformed into the likeness of Christ's own. Such bodies are not subject to the weaknesses and limitations of our current forms, which are made of perishable flesh and blood. Sickness and disease, even death, will have no effect on such bodies. From the biblical accounts of Christ's post-resurrection visits to the gathered apostles, we know that His body was no longer confined to the laws of physics as we understand them: He could appear and disappear at will, even in and out of closed and locked rooms. Yet, He remained recognizable to the apostles.

Glorification also includes the elevation of believers to the status of Christ as heir and ruler of God's creation. Thus, they shall live in the New Jerusalem, the city of light, in the presence of God for eternity!

* * *

As much as salvation is freely given to mankind, it comes with responsibilities that must be understood and embraced in God's own terms. As elaborated throughout the preceding chapters, one who comes to Christ must understand those responsibilities and accept them on his or her own free will. The whole purpose of the gospel is to communicate the truth of those responsibilities and the entailing opportunity costs to the unbeliever so that the decision to believe is made with serenity and full understanding of what it means to live the Christian life. So, how well have we been doing to assume our responsibilities as believers? The following chapter will take a closer look at and expound on the related practices.

CHAPTER 8

A House Built on Sand

And Jesus came and spoke to them, saying, "All authority has been given to Me in heaven and on earth. Go therefore and make disciples of all the nations, baptizing them in the name of the Father and of the Son and of the Holy Spirit, teaching them to observe all things that I have commanded you; and lo, I am with you always, even to the end of the age. (Matthew 28:18-20 NKJV)

These are the words of Jesus Christ, collectively known in Christian circles as the "Great Commission." They form the biblical foundation for all Christian ministries and missions around the world.

The statements of the Great Commission are straightforward compared to Jesus' prior teachings, which were often expressed in parables. Nevertheless, some subtle aspects of His message often escape our understanding. First, it is important to consider the Lord's audience while He uttered those words. He was speaking to the eleven remaining apostles—men who *believed in* Him and had spent the last two and a half years learning not only about God through the person of His Son but also how to live life as Jesus did on Earth, both physically and spiritually.

Similar to most apprenticeship programs, the Great Commission comprises two essential aspects: (1) the theoretical knowledge through hearing the spoken words of the master and (2) the life discipline developed from observing and practicing the master's way of life. Both aspects are critical for the apprentice to learn and develop a character and lifestyle in the likeness of the master.

The theoretical knowledge explains the training practices and provides the reasons why they are necessary and beneficial, whereas the training practices teach the apprentice how to apply the theoretical knowledge to reap the resulting benefits. Without theoretical knowledge, the apprentice would lack insight into the master's way of life and would not understand the importance of the training practices taught by the master. Conversely, without opportunities to observe the master in action and practice his or her way of life, all the acquired theoretical knowledge would not yield practical benefits for the apprentice. Therefore, in a training program, it is crucial for both the master and the apprentice to be fully committed to both theoretical knowledge and training practices if there is any hope for the apprentice to develop into the likeness of the master. Christian discipleship is no exception.

Biblical knowledge and the practice of life according to biblical principles are equally critical. Without a preacher—one who imparts theoretical knowledge—no one will hear the gospel of Jesus Christ.

How can they believe in Him of whom they have not heard? And how can they hear unless someone preaches (Romans 10:14)? However, how can they observe the commands of Christ unless someone demonstrates for them how it is practically done in daily life?

Great Commission: The Original Command

The Great Commission is the Lord Jesus' command to His disciples to go all over the world and preach the gospel. However, the all-knowing Lord did not instruct them to go and *only* preach. He said: "Teaching them to observe all things that I have commanded you," meaning they were to not only preach but also to teach those who come to believe how to practice everything He had taught them during the two and a half years they spent together. Note that the Lord Jesus lived, traveled, ministered, ate, slept, laughed, and sometimes cried with these same disciples. He spoke to them; they listened to His parables and sermons; they asked Him questions, and He explained what they did not readily understand. He knew the disciples' life struggles and helped them through.

They also learned about Jesus' life as He shared His experiences with them. In fact, He called them "friends," reasoning that they were not servants because servants do not know the master's business (John 15:14-15). That is how close the Lord Jesus was to His disciples. It was essential for them to not only learn about their master but also to embrace and practice His way of life; to learn how to think like Him and to be concerned with His interests as they were with their own. They needed to be present to witness Him restore sight to the blind, give speech to the mute, provide health to the sick,

79

and yes, bring life to the dead! They needed Him to empower them to perform miracles when He sent them on short mission trips. The disciples did not have the indwelling of the Holy Spirit yet—they only received Him at Pentecost, after the Lord Jesus rose from the dead and ascended into heaven. Until then, the disciples could not produce any spiritual fruit without Jesus.

Great Commission: The Current Practice

Today, those who have the megaphones to preach the gospel have mostly turned its message into a means to ultimately enrich themselves. Let me explain: institutionalizing the churches has resulted in those in leadership worrying more about the numbers than the spiritual well-being of those who attend services in the church buildings. The size of the congregation is the church's measuring stick for success. So, the truth of Christ's message of salvation is diluted, overlooked, and sometimes outright distorted to appeal to the masses while the truth of the gospel and the tenets of the resulting Christian life get lost in the shuffle.

I am saddened to say that, as common as those practices are today, their results are disastrous: the large majority of unbelievers perceive the church as a scheme established by its leaders to exploit their weak and naïve neighbors. Christians are mostly seen as hypocrites who talk the talk but never walk the walk.

The institutionalized churches are certainly very lucrative for those who founded and have been leading them—at least in this life—but the end will be even more disastrous for those leaders.

You might be silently saying to yourself, "We send hundreds of thousands of missionaries all over the world; we spend millions of our money to support them so they can preach the gospel; we have planted myriads of churches around the globe. In our churches, we preach, we have discipleship programs, we minister; we are fulfilling the Great Commission." You speak the truth, for such ministries are being conducted in the local churches and all over the world. Nevertheless, they are failing to produce the expected fruit in our families, neighborhoods, cities, and countries.

Despite all the Sunday schooling, youth ministries, and vacation Bible schooling, many of the children of our church founders and leaders have deserted or are deserting their childhood churches, stepping farther away from the faith of their parents, proving that they never had it. Among those, some have turned to debauchery in rebellion against the claimed faith of their parents. The majority of the congregants in most churches are fifty years of age or older. The young people are nowhere to be found.

Many believers who used to faithfully attend church on Sundays no longer do. Isn't it about time for us to start asking and seeking answers to the hard questions? Why have the children of the believers left and are still leaving the church in droves? Why aren't all the ministries, missions, and church programs bearing the expected spiritual fruits? Why do more and more believers no longer believe in the institutionalized church? Can the tides be reversed against the exodus of believers from churches? Why is the church powerless against the loss of the potential next generation of Christians around the world?

We will attempt to unveil some of the root causes of the challenges facing today's church and provide some answers to the heart-wrenching questions in the following chapter, starting with the institutional nucleus of the church: that is, the family.

CHAPTER 9

Walking the Talk

The family is the nucleus of the church: the Lord appointed it as the upbringing environment and training ground for the next generation of Christians (Malachi 2:15). Contrary to the popular tendency to delegate the teaching of children to church programs, the Lord lays that responsibility on the parents. It is a big responsibility that entails relentless prayers, teaching, question-and-answer sessions, and modeling the practices of Christian life for the children. The responsibility is challenging but possible for parents engaged in a biblically sound marriage relationship. So, let us start our analysis of the issues there.

The Essence of Biblical Marriage

Marriage is perhaps one of the most misunderstood institutions in Christian circles, and there are numerous reasons for that. First and foremost, marriage has always existed within secular societies. As a result, the pre-existing secular views of marriage, which often pre-date those of Christianity, remain ingrained in the perspectives of married Christians living in those societies.

Across the world, even within the same country, Christians often have diverging views on marriage. Second, the standards of a biblical marriage are often contrary to those of traditional marriages in many cultures. Consequently, Christians from conflicting cultural backgrounds may uphold their secular views of marriage even after conversion unless they are taught otherwise. Some spouses enter marriage with their own preconceived ideas and visions of what it should be. These ideas and visions often conflict with those of the other spouse, and frequently with the biblical standards of marriage; these are some of the initial sources of tension.

Third, prospective Christian couples undergoing premarital counseling quickly learn that divorce will not be an acceptable option for resolving marital differences. What is often lacking is education on the fundamentals of a joyful, lifelong, loving, and biblical marriage relationship where divorce is not even a thought, not because the spouses are coerced to dismiss the idea, but because they cherish their relationship to the point where they can hardly envision a better life without each other.

Fourth, as the church experiences more and more political, secular, and cultural pressures, the standards of its institutions, including marriage, are gradually shifting away from their original foundations. The lines between the concepts of Christian and secular marriage are becoming increasingly blurred, even though the biblical teachings that define the Christian standards of marriage remain unchanged. Nevertheless, marriage is such a solemn undertaking that it is essential for Christians engaged in it and those desiring to marry to fully understand its biblical meaning, what God's expectations are for married Christian couples, and the responsibilities prescribed by God that accompany Christian marriage. To gain insights into the biblical concept of marriage, let's analyze it in light of relevant scriptures, beginning with the divine purpose for the institution.

The Divine Purpose of Marriage

Besides a person's commitment to follow Jesus Christ, marriage is arguably the second most life-changing relationship one can engage in throughout a lifetime. Whether joyful or heart-wrenching, the impact of marriage on the lives of the spouses and their children is undeniable. Every aspect of one's being is influenced by marriage: it affects the mind, heart, body, soul, and spirit. Both spouses must be completely vulnerable to each other in a marriage that adheres to biblical standards. There is truly no room for prenuptial agreements, separate bank accounts, or similar arrangements. We will revisit a detailed examination of these implications and their effects in a later section of this chapter.

From a biblical perspective, marriage is intended to be a lifetime commitment, by a male and a female to love each other in every way, to provide companionship, erotic love, agape love, and brotherly love, as well as to raise godly offspring for God. Let's examine these aspects of marriage in light of the relevant biblical principles.

Erotic Love in Marriage

This is perhaps the most primitive form of love expressed by all married couples, Christians and non-Christians alike. From a biblical point of view, marriage reaches far beyond the basic "animal" instinct of erotic love, into the spiritual life of the mind, the heart, and the soul. Erotic love has its place in the spiritual life of a married couple.

In 1 Corinthians 7:3-6, the apostle Paul makes the following state-ment as a concession to the insistent inquiries from the Corinthians on this very subject:

> Let the husband render to his wife the affection due her, and likewise also the wife to her husband. The wife does not have authority over her own body, but the husband does. And like-wise the husband does not have authority over his own body, but the wife does. Do not deprive one another except with consent for a time, that you may give yourselves to fasting and prayer; and come together again so that Satan does not tempt you because of your lack of self-control. But I say this as a concession, not as a commandment. (NKJV)

This is the apostle's opinion because he says so himself; neverthe-less, it is grounded in biblical wisdom imparted by the Holy Spirit. There are three key points to be retained from this passage:

1. A spouse *"does not have authority over"* his or her own body. That is, neither the wife nor the husband can do what-ever, wherever, whenever, and however they want with their own body without the consent of the other spouse. It does not say that the husband can force his wife into the sexual act within a marriage. Neither does it say that the wife can

use her body as a means to manipulate and bring her husband into submission. On the contrary, the passage is advising each spouse to willingly *"render ... the affection due"* to the other spouse.

2. When necessary, as it may be when fasting and praying, each spouse must agree to abstain from the sexual act *"for a time"* in order to focus on God. However, such a time period must not be unnecessarily prolonged so that the spouse lacking self-control may be relieved and not fall into temptation from Satan.

3. Paul explicitly states that what he is writing in this passage is his response to former inquiries, not a command from the Lord.

With respect to the first key point, a husband might think that he is being granted authority to force his wife into the sexual act because he has authority over her body. That is shortsighted because in doing so, he forgets that his own body is under his wife's authority and, as a result, he is not to use it in any manner without her consent. Likewise, the wife is not to deprive her husband of the sexual act. The point is that it takes consent from both spouses to engage in the sexual act if they are going to live by the principles conveyed in the passage. This is crucial because erotic love in marriage is meant to be an expression of affection: the affection that the spouses vowed to give each other on their wedding day. More importantly, it keeps the spouses' affections and desires focused on each other, which helps against distractions that are likely to lead to temptations. For that reason, any practice that is disapproved of by one spouse must not be applied. Such practices could lead to emotional distress, desensitization, resentment, etc., between the couple: The offensive spouse runs the risk of becoming obnoxious, rude, selfish, and unlikable to the other, turning the very act that is meant to bring about closeness and unity into a destructive factor, undermining whatever level of unity ever existed.

Such situations thwart the oneness of the couple, which can hinder their prayers at best or ultimately lead to separation and divorce at worst. Coercing a spouse into the sexual act violates the non-consenting spouse's conscience, giving Satan a foot in the door to lead the couple into temptation, which brings us to the second point of the passage.

The passage makes room for exceptional situations where accommodations must be made. Spouses must be compassionate and understanding with each other — that should not be unbearably hard to do if they indeed have *agape* love for one another. There may be situations where a spouse is unable to physically grant his or her affection to the other for very good reasons. In such cases, it is incumbent on the other spouse to be loving, understanding, supportive, and enduring so as not to lose self-control. The lack of sex has never killed anyone. The enduring spouse should go to the Lord with their grievances in prayer, ask for His strength, His peace—which surpasses understanding—and He will see them through.

Someone desiring to continue the former sexual practices into a Christian marriage may argue that the apostle Paul's statements are not commands and therefore don't necessarily need to be applied to their marriage. Nevertheless, in Galatians 5:19, Paul also writes: "Now the works of the flesh are evident, which are: adultery, fornication, uncleanness, lewdness" (NKJV), and we know that uncleanness, lewdness, and adultery or fornication are not synonyms. He also writes in Ephesians 5:3, "But fornication and all uncleanness or covetousness, let it not even be named among you, as is fitting for saints" (NKJV). It goes without saying that uncleanness and lewdness should not be pursued or continued by couples after their conversion to Christianity. The related sexual practices can lead to:

1. Violation of the conscience of a spouse
2. Abusive acts towards a spouse
3. Impropriety and indecency

They can also turn sex, which is a natural expression of affection between spouses, into an abusive act that erodes their attraction and likability for one another. For believers, sex within marriage should not be an occasion for the former shameful and worldly practices, as when they did not know the Lord; such practices do not become approved by the Lord because they are being perpetuated by those who claim to bear His name. Instead, believers ought to walk in the light:

> For you were once darkness, but now you are light in the Lord. Walk as children of light (for the fruit of the Spirit is in all goodness, righteousness, and truth), finding out what is acceptable to the Lord. And have no fellowship with the unfruitful works of darkness but rather expose them. For it

is shameful even to speak of those things which are done by them in secret. (Ephesians 5:8-12 NKJV).

Sex is great, but it is only part of the story, so let's continue our exploration of the spiritual aspects of marriage.

Companionship in Marriage

The spiritual nature of companionship may come as a surprise at first. However, companionship is divine. We humans are alone within ourselves, but God is not: the Bible teaches us that the Christian God is a Trinity; that is, a being made up of three distinct personalities who coexist in perfect harmony: the Father, the Son, and the Holy Spirit. If that is not the ultimate companionship, I don't know what is! In fact, companionship is so spiritually foundational that it influenced creation from the very beginning. It is even integral to God's view of what is good.

The book of Genesis recounts that, besides mankind, the Lord God looked at His living creation and declared it good. However, concerning mankind, He said:

> It is not good that man should be alone; I will make him a helper comparable to him... And the Lord God caused a deep sleep to fall on Adam, and he slept; and He took one of his ribs, and closed up the flesh in its place. Then the rib which the Lord God had taken from man He made into a woman, and He brought her to the man. (Genesis 2:18, 2:21 NKJV).

Needless to say, the companionship between a man and his wife has been a divine objective since the beginning. God created the woman (Eve) from the man (Adam) to establish a strong bond between the two from the start.

He indeed created the first family in the image of the perfect oneness of the Trinity. Thus, companionship is a divinely ordained aspect of Christian marriage. As such, it is the duty of each spouse in a Christian marriage to actively contribute to the fulfillment of God's will by providing an enjoyable, supportive, and united partnership for the other spouse. Of course, this is impossible without genuine peace, harmony, and mutual respect between the spouses. Therefore, they must prioritize quickly resolving differences that arise in daily life, understanding each other, genuinely caring for one another, and anticipating and meeting each other's needs as much as possible.

Spouses must make a concerted effort to live as a unit and not as the bachelor and bachelorette they once were, consulting, listening, and heeding each other while making decisions that directly or indirectly affect the family or their relationship. They must forsake old habits or lifestyles that create forces susceptible to pulling them apart and reinforce those that nurture the well-being of the unit. Spouses who practice these principles genuinely enjoy each other's company and prefer to engage in activities together. In fact, they find activities less enjoyable when their spouses are not participants.

Clearly, the companionship envisioned by the Creator cannot exist as a standalone feature of marriage. It is a necessary aspect of marriage, but it is certainly not sufficient. The decision to marry also entails a commitment from each spouse to look after the interests of the other in the same way he or she looks after his or her own interests, regardless of external circumstances. That is a commitment to love each other with agape love.

Agape Love in Marriage

Recalling the earlier chapter on the biblical concepts of love, *agape* is a willful decision by the lover to prioritize the personal interests of the beloved. It is not a feeling-driven response. The biblical standards for marriage elevate the level of commitment in that decision to one of life and death. In Ephesians 5:25-28, the apostle Paul writes:

> Husbands, love your wives, just as Christ loved the church and gave himself up for her to make her holy, cleansing her by the washing with water through the word, and to present her to himself as a radiant church, without stain or wrinkle or any other blemish, but holy and blameless. In this same way, husbands ought to love their wives as their own bodies. He who loves his wife loves himself... For this reason a man will leave his father and mother and be united to his wife, and the two will become one flesh. (NIV)

There are three noteworthy points concerning marriage in this passage: (1) A husband must detach from the authority of his father and mother and free himself in order to enter into a relationship as deep and engaging as the one he previously had with them, namely, marriage. (2) A husband must care for the personal interests of his wife—which includes providing for her in every possible way—to the point of being willing to die loving her, just as Jesus Christ loved the Church to the extent of offering himself as a sacrifice for her redemption. (3) The golden rule—"You shall love your neighbor as yourself"—emphatically applies to husbands in a Christian marriage.

Regarding wives, the apostle Paul also writes in Ephesians 5:22-24, "Wives, submit yourselves to your own husbands as you do to the Lord. For the husband is the head of the wife as Christ is the head of the church, his body, of which he is the Savior. Now as the church submits to Christ, so also wives should submit to their husbands in everything" (NIV).

The key point concerning wives is *submission*. It is important to emphasize that this is not a license for husbands to coerce their wives into submission. It is a command for wives to submit to their husbands of their own volition as part of their reverence for the Lord.

The passage assigns a role to each spouse in the marriage to establish order. A Christian wife cannot compel her husband to love her in the biblically prescribed manner; neither can a Christian husband force his wife into submission in the biblical way. The Lord is a God of order and truth, who only deals in truth. Thus, any scheme devised to coerce a spouse into behaving according to biblical standards undermines its purpose. A wife submits to her husband, and her husband loves her because they are both believers; they love the Lord and eagerly seek to live in His will, and as a result, His Spirit empowers them to do so.

The key points from the biblical standards of marriage are foundational: a marriage cannot meet the biblical standards without them. They are also the areas where many marriages fail; hence our need to examine them in the social context, starting with the notion of "leaving parents and uniting with wives."

Leaving Parents and Uniting with a Wife

In some cultures, a man never leaves his father's house; the expectation is for him to marry and bring his wife there. The parents and siblings expect no changes in the relationships they have with their son or brother after he marries. They expect him to prioritize their interests over those of his wife. In other words, they expect him to love his wife less than the Bible requires of him. The wife is viewed and sometimes treated as an outsider by her in-laws, who often despise her and her birth family members, whom they view as strangers constantly seeking to profit from their son or brother. Under these pressures, a weak husband often leaves his wife to the mercy of his birth family members, who dislike her for one reason or another.

In matriarchal cultures, the children are often viewed as heirs to their maternal family, not as legitimate beneficiaries of the husband's livelihood. Thus, the very biblical requirement for a husband to provide for his wife and children stirs up strife! As a result, such a husband often remains attached to his birth family more than he would otherwise be to his wife. In some other cultures, a husband who leaves his birth family to be joined to his wife is socially viewed as a lesser man; a man who has been "wrapped around his wife's little finger"—so to speak. A mother often blames and despises her son's wife, whom she sees as an oppressor of her son.

Regardless of the social background, the dread of in-laws, especially mothers-in-law, seems to be universal, and its effects on marriages do not spare Christian couples. Either the husband's mother does not approve of her daughter-in-law, or the wife's mother does not think that the husband is a man worthy of her daughter; and the list of reasons goes on.

We Christian parents must understand that supporting and facilitating our sons' and daughters' marriages, the biblical way, is part of our responsibility to love our neighbor as ourselves. The Lord gave us the children as a result of marriages with other people's sons and daughters. We must be willing to do for others what has already been done for us.

Loving a Wife as Christ Loved the Church
This is where most husbands in Christian marriages struggle. This is not about emotional feelings for one's wife; it is a conscientious commitment to care for her needs, even those she may not know about.

Agape love is a choice; if we can make that choice for our enemies as the Lord commands us (Matthew 5:43-44), it could not possibly be harder to make that same choice for our wives! However, the depth of agape love biblically required from a husband for his wife goes beyond that commanded toward his enemies. The Scriptures don't command us to die for our enemies. They do command the husband to love his wife to the point of being willing to die defending her personal interests. This is really the same as the husband loving his wife as himself. Any person would be willing to die defending their own interests if it came to a matter of life and death.

It is important to note that a husband who possesses this level of love for his wife does not act as a dictator. He is gentle with her; he cares about her feelings, her opinion regarding how he leads the family, and the actions he undertakes for the benefit of the family. Perhaps this is the depth of love that must be demonstrated for a woman to feel reassured of her safety in total submission to her husband?

Regardless of the reason for this command, the Lord knows best, and if husbands truly believe in Him, they should not hesitate to love their wives in the biblical way, in obedience to His Word. This is not to say that it is easy; we have already discussed the various obstacles that Christian husbands face in marriage. Nevertheless, we must make tough choices and obey the Lord regardless of the consequences. That is faith.

Total Submission to a Husband
Many Christian women struggle with the matter of total submission

to their husbands, and for good reasons. First, a husband who is not willing to love his wife to the level commanded by the Scriptures should not expect her to find him trustworthy enough to feel secure in totally submitting to him. Second, the social norms of the day totally contradict the idea of a woman fully submitting to her husband.

Given the historically oppressive practices of men toward women, this social reaction to counterbalance male dominance is justified. However, cultural values and belief systems must not be elevated to the level of God's true Word. We are not talking here about the many warped interpretations of the biblical text taught by those with personal agendas. We are referring to the unbiased truth as expressed in the Scriptures. Thus, women are commanded to submit to their own husbands as the church submits to the Lord Jesus Christ. Note that the believer's submission to the Lord is not by coercion.

We freely choose to submit to Him because we love and believe in Him. That love and belief are not blind either. We know who He is and how He has demonstrated His love for us to the point of death on a Roman cross to save us from the eternal agony of hell. Therefore, we feel secure trusting Him with our lives.

My point is that husbands cannot make wives truly submit to them in the way prescribed in the Scriptures. They can coerce them to adopt desired patterns of behavior, but that kind of fake submission is not what the Lord wants. Remember that He sees through all falsehood and treachery. The true submission that He requires of Christian wives must be given of their own free will, without any coercion or similar pressures.

Brotherly Love in Marriage

We rarely, if ever, think of a spouse as a brother or sister in the secular and cultural sense, but brotherly love plays a role in Christian marriages. As the well-known adage puts it, "blood is thicker than water." Christian couples who strive to live by biblical standards become one flesh according to the Scriptures. They develop brotherly love for each other. That is one aspect of their marriage that makes them tolerant, never thinking of permanently departing from each other as a means of problem resolution.

There is an African saying that likens a fight between siblings to a hot water drop on someone's skin; it burns and hurts intensely, but the pain only lasts for a short while. So, too, are disagreements between siblings who truly have brotherly love for each other. They disagree but then quickly come together to talk and resolve their differences. That is an important practice in Christian marriage as well because the spouses are brother and sister in the Lord.

Those desiring to marry the biblical way may be asking themselves how to avoid the pitfalls of marriage discussed in the preceding sections of this chapter. So, I will attempt to provide some advice based on my biblical insight and personal experience with marriage.

Knowing that a house built on sand cannot stand the storm, let's start with the foundational aspects that create a stable and durable marriage relationship.

Values and Worldview

Marriage is like a team sport. There can be no wins unless each player espouses the game strategy established by the coach and plays his or her part to contribute to the team's efforts. In a Christian marriage, the coach is God; the players are the spouses; the game plan is established and conveyed to the players by God's Word as taught through Scripture. For the marriage to thrive, it is critical that the spouses be in agreement concerning life-impacting decisions.

Unfortunately, Christian spouses, like most believers, rarely have the same level of understanding of Scripture or spiritual maturity. There lies the main source of divergence in opinions and points of view between the Christian spouses. Teachers in the church would effectively help the situation if they would stick to teaching the truth and nothing but the truth of the Word of God on the subject matter. However, we know from our discussion of Christian ministry in the earlier chapters that the truth is rarely taught. Nevertheless, it is absolutely necessary for the health of a Christian marriage that both spouses come to know and agree with the Word of God by faith.

Both spouses must be committed to obedience to the Word of God, at least as it pertains to marriage. Regardless of the level of love that each spouse may feel for the other, there are always going to be life situations where the spouses will have diverging points of view, and that will put the marriage relationship to the test. A spouse may believe in the authority of their biological parents, overriding the other spouse's points of view, whereas the other spouse does not.

The husband may believe in the wife's submission to his position of authority, whereas the wife does not. The wife may believe in her husband loving her the biblical way, whereas the husband, oblivious to the related biblical truths, may prioritize his own interests above hers, etc. It is in those situations that the aligned beliefs become essential to reaching a consensual resolution of matters. In those instances, the authority of the Word of God supplants the spouses' individual opinions, and what it says is ultimately accepted by both parties because they are believers.

The ultimate resolutions of some of these situations can significantly impact the life of the family. As a result, they are not easily accepted by the spouses unless an agreement can be reached. More often than not, the situation would otherwise turn into a war of opinions and remain unresolved without the safety net of God's Word. The differences arising from such situations can easily fester and create a wedge between the spouses, an attack on the oneness prescribed by the Word of God concerning marriage.

Needless to say, having common biblical truth-based values and worldviews is a critical component of healthy Christian marriages. Those seeking such relationships ought to seriously consider that as a necessary criterion when choosing a potential spouse. That is the reason why it is important for a believer to marry another believer.

Note that I am using the term "believer" to reference someone who believes in Christ, not one who only claims to be a Christian. The distinction is very important because most of the aspects of marriage discussed in this chapter would not work for unbelievers.

The apostle Paul emphasizes this point of conflict in marriages where one of the spouses is an unbeliever. He urges Christians not to marry unbelievers because they will have troubles due to their conflicting ways of life. In his letter to the Corinthians, he writes:

> Do not be unequally yoked together with unbelievers. For what fellowship has righteousness with lawlessness? And what communion has light with darkness? And what accord has Christ with Belial? Or what part has a believer with an unbeliever? And what agreement has the temple of God with idols? For you are the temple of the living God. As God has said: 'I will dwell in them and walk among them. I will be their God, and they shall be My people.' Therefore 'Come out from among them and be separate, says the Lord. Do not touch what is unclean, and I will receive you.' 'I will be a Father to you, And you shall be My sons and daughters, Says the Lord Almighty.' (2 Corinthians 6:14-18 NKJV)

What is Paul's point? Is marrying an unbeliever a sin? No, not in itself. However, it is likely to create situations of conflict that make the believing spouse's life very difficult if he or she is to live a holy and sanctified life. The unbeliever still lives in darkness according to the above passage. As a result, he or she is most likely to continue the practices inherent to that life, whereas the Lord calls the believer to walk away from the worldly lifestyle and its practices to live a holy life.

This conflict exists:

> For the flesh lusts against the Spirit, and the Spirit against the flesh; and these are contrary to one another, so that you do not do the things that you wish. But if you are led by the Spirit, you are not under the law. Now the works of the flesh are evident, which are: adultery, fornication, uncleanness, lewdness, idolatry, sorcery, hatred, contentions, jealousies, outbursts of wrath, selfish ambitions, dissensions, heresies, envy, murders, drunkenness, revelries, and the like; of which I tell you beforehand, just as I also told you in time past, that those who practice such things will not inherit the kingdom of God. But the fruit of the Spirit is love, joy, peace, long-suffering, kindness, goodness, faithfulness, gentleness, self-control. Against such there is no law. And those who are Christ's have crucified the flesh with its passions and desires. (Galatians 5:17-24 NKJV)

The follow-up and logical question for readers already engaged in marriage is: "What to do if my spouse will not take heed to the Word of God?" I see two answers depending on the circumstances: if your spouse knows the biblical truth concerning the matter at hand and yet consciously chooses to disobey God, there is nothing more you can physically do to change the situation. At that point, I would consider the rebellious spouse as an unbeliever who has no intention of staying in marriage with you, and settle the matter accordingly. The apostle Paul dealt with that case in 1 Corinthians 7:13-16, where he writes:

> And a woman who has a husband who does not believe, if he is willing to live with her, let her not divorce him. For the unbelieving husband is sanctified by the wife, and the unbelieving wife is sanctified by the husband; otherwise your children would be unclean, but now they are holy. But if the unbeliever departs, let him depart; a brother or a sister is not under bondage in such cases. But God has called us to peace. For how do you know, O wife, whether you will save your husband? Or how do you know, O husband, whether you will save your wife? (NKJV)

In cases where the dissenting spouse is genuinely ignorant of the truth, the knowledgeable or spiritually more mature spouse must pray for the enlightenment of the other while gracefully engaging him or her in Scripture-based discussions of the relevant biblical principles. Such discussions must be objective and Scripture-based to be effective and minimize, possibly eliminate, disagreements anchored in personal opinions; only God's opinion matters, after all. The good news is that two believers in genuine pursuit of the will of God concerning a matter will always find it (John 9:31; Matthew 7:7-11).

Now, not every situation in a marriage calls for such seriousness: there are diverging opinions on non-spiritually impeding matters. The fact of the matter is that two imperfect beings with shared interests in all aspects of life will sometimes disagree. The good news is that the underlying matters of such disagreements typically arise from unimportant cultural and character differences without spiritual significance.

The love between Christian couples who live by biblical principles can overshadow and dissipate such disagreements because agape "love is patient, love is kind. It does not envy, it does not boast, it is not proud. It does not dishonor others, it is not self-seeking, it is not easily angered, it keeps no record of wrongs. Love does not delight in evil but rejoices with the truth. It always protects, always trusts, always hopes, always perseveres" (1 Corinthians 13:4-6 NIV).

This is where wives are called to be humble and submit to their husbands of their own volition, not because they are compelled to do so. In the same way, husbands, you are called to "be considerate as you live with your wives, and treat them with respect as the weaker partner and as heirs with you of the gracious gift of life, so that nothing will hinder your prayers" (1 Peter 3:7 NIV).

Goodly Offsprings in Marriage

What does God expect from Christian couples pertaining to their marriage? Contrary to today's popular practice of depending on church programs, Christian schools, and similar institutions for the

Christian education of the children, God has placed that responsibility with the parents. Yes, it is our personal responsibility to teach our children in the ways of the Lord, not anyone else's. It just makes common sense that the infinitely wise Creator, who invented marriage, would assign that responsibility to the parents. They are supposed to be the ones who spend most of the hours in a day with their children.

All the institutions to which the Christian education of the children has been outsourced do not have the needed time or environment to effectively perform that duty. Churches only have the children for a couple of hours each week, and the focus of Christian schools is mostly on secular education with a sprinkle of bits and pieces of Christian ideology. Being a believer does not consist of memorizing Bible verses or accumulating knowledge about God; it is not an activity that one performs; it is a way of life. As such, the process of making disciples — aka true believers—includes two essential components: (1) teaching principles, and (2) teaching how to live by the taught principles. As in any practical training, repetition is essential in the latter aspect of the process of making believers.

Believe it or not, raising children in the ways of the Lord is meant to be a Christian ministry. The family is the mission field; the potential converts are the children, and the missionaries are the parents. A divine purpose of the marriage environment, as prescribed by the Bible, is meant to bring up godly offspring (Malachi 2:15). That is not possible unless someone diligently teaches and models the related Christian practices to the children. Children do not do what their parents tell them to do; they do what they see their parents do.

Unfortunately, children born to believing parents do not automatically believe; they must be preached and taught the gospel just like any other unbelieving people. They often have pointed questions that must be logically answered. Telling them to blindly believe something just because Dad or Mom says so does not go past elementary school.

I vividly recall my daughter questioning me about the theory of evolution in fourth grade. We engaged in a logical discussion of the subject, and she quickly came to realize that the arguments for the theory soon fell apart under scrutiny. I did not have to quote a single Bible verse in that discussion, but I effectively conveyed the fact that evolution is a theory and should only be viewed as such. My point is that you do not have to be a seminary graduate to provide a Christian education to your children. I probably would not trust them with my children anyway, unless I knew them personally to be true believers, not professional ministers.

The integrity and faithfulness that you demonstrate with your life for Christ, along with your sharing of learned biblical principles with your children, is what is needed. To effectively teach their children, parents must learn by studying the Scriptures, which is the responsibility of all believers, whether they are parents or not. It is almost impossible for anyone to grow and mature in the knowledge of Christ without personally studying the Word of God.

Please do not misunderstand my statements. I am not talking about attending a Bible study where you get lectures from a teacher without opportunities to ask the hard questions for fear of being black-listed as a heretic. Seek Bible studies where teachers are open-minded enough to discuss related matters and answer questions with biblically grounded logical arguments. Ponder on the Scriptures on your own and pray that the Holy Spirit enlightens you on the matters that you do not understand.

I know from personal experience that the Lord will reveal His will to you if you seek it in order to do it (Jeremiah 29:13; James 4:8; John 7:17). If you want your children to be believers, you must embrace your God-assigned responsibility and assume it as a service to the Lord.

This is not to say that parents who assume their God-assigned responsibility of raising their children in the ways of the Lord are guaranteed to have offspring that are all believers. Belief in Christ is first and foremost an individual choice that parents cannot make for their children. The Lord only calls them to do their part in leading their children's hearts to Him.

Some parents may claim that they are not good with children, and that may be true to some extent, but it always comes to this: the children do what they see their parents do. If the parents live godly lives to earn the trust and respect of their children, they are more likely to keep walking in the paths set before them. Outsourcing the upbringing of the children to the church is far from being an answer. Most of those conducting children's ministries in churches are not more gifted than parents in the area of child-rearing. The discourse of spiritual gifts in the following chapter sheds some light on the matter.

CHAPTER 10

Spiritual Gifts and Christian Ministry

First Corinthians 12 makes it abundantly clear that spiritual gifts are given to believers by the Lord Jesus through the Holy Spirit. With the exception of Jesus Christ Himself, who had the Spirit within Him at conception, no other human has ever been born with the Holy Spirit residing inside. In fact, no one but God knows when a believer is indwelled by the Holy Spirit.

In the conversion recorded in John Chapter 3, the Lord Jesus said to Nicodemus: "The wind blows where it wishes, and you hear the sound of it, but cannot tell where it comes from and where it goes. So is everyone who is born of the Spirit." In other words, we can only perceive the workings of the Holy Spirit in the life of a born-again Christian by their observable effects. We don't know how they begin or what patterns they follow. What, then, is a spiritual gift?

The essence of the aforementioned conversation is that humans are not born with spiritual gifts because they are granted by the Holy Spirit to believers, and the Bible teaches us that no human is a believer at natural birth. Therefore, we can confidently conclude that secular skills, which are possessed by an individual at natural birth, cannot possibly be spiritual gifts.

To my knowledge—and I have extensively searched the Scriptures on this topic—there is no biblical basis for the popular belief that an individual's natural skills, arising from fleshly abilities, turn into spiritual gifts at conversion. That is not to say that one's spiritual gift can never coincide with a natural ability. However, remembering that the Holy Spirit is not a spirit of disorder or confusion, I would argue that such coincidences are not the norm.

The Scriptures instruct us to test every spirit (Matthew 7:15-20; 1 John 4:1). We must, therefore, judge every gift by its fruit, assessing whether it bears spiritual fruit before concluding that it is a spiritual gift.

A spiritual gift is an empowering of the gifted by the indwelling gift-giver, the Holy Spirit. Its perceptible manifestation is solely the result of the Holy Spirit working in the gifted. As such, the spiritual gift and the Giver are inseparable. The spiritual gift cannot, and does not, exist apart from the Holy Spirit. We should also note that unless a life is led by the Holy Spirit, the Spirit cannot manifest within it. This is because the Spirit never forces Himself onto anyone: unless a person is willing to follow the Spirit, he cannot be led by the Spirit.

We don't have the ability to see into the human heart, but we have been granted spiritual wisdom to discern and differentiate the spiritual from the carnal. Truly spirit-led lives are characterized by the fruit of the Spirit, which consists of "love, joy, peace, longsuffering, kindness, goodness, faithfulness, gentleness, self-control" (Galatians 5:22-23 NKJV). These are character traits obviously visible in lives that are truly led by the Holy Spirit, and it is in those lives that spiritual gifts can be manifested.

This is not to say that all abilities of a spirit-led believer are spiritual gifts. The natural abilities of such a believer do not disappear or automatically transform into spiritual gifts at conversion. Of course, a natural ability that coincides with a spiritual gift may appear as though it has been converted, but it should not be confused with the superimposed spiritual gift.

A natural ability that does not coincide with a spiritual gift will remain distinctly fleshly and incapable of producing spiritual fruit in ministry: "That which is born of the flesh is flesh, and that which is born of the Spirit is spirit" (John 3:6). Therefore, it is paramount for those engaged in church ministry to fully understand this if they desire spiritual fruit in their communities, including their church members to whom they minister. Since the purpose of spiritual gifts is Christian ministry, ministers must truly understand what it means from a biblical perspective. So, what is the essence of Christian ministry?

The Essence of Christian Ministry
Genuine Christian ministry is the use of a believer's spiritual gift to perform work *solely* purposed for nurturing other Christians to spiritual maturity. Its sole objective is the growth of Christians to the

full knowledge of Christ (Ephesians 4:7-16); that is, full spiritual maturity. It is the state of mind where the believer knows the truth and has the power of discernment to distinguish what is true from what is false Christian doctrine, among other qualities (Ephesians 4:13-16). Genuine Christian ministry is exclusively motivated by the minister's love for Christ and those being nurtured—nothing more, nothing less. I dare say that any added fleshly motive turns Christian ministry into a sinful performance of which the Lord Jesus wants no part.

In the following passage, the Lord Jesus is rebuking false ministers for using His name to pursue their personal agendas:

> Not everyone who says to Me, 'Lord, Lord,' shall enter the kingdom of heaven, but he who does the will of My Father in heaven. Many will say to Me in that day, 'Lord, Lord, have we not prophesied in Your name, cast out demons in Your name, and done many wonders in Your name?' And then I will declare to them, 'I never knew you; depart from Me, you who practice lawlessness!' (Matthew 7:21-23 NKJV)

Note that the Lord is not disputing the veracity of the claims to have used His name to prophesy, cast out demons, or perform miracles because those ministers indeed did those things. He is refuting their claim to have done so in His name because, in reality, their performance was motivated by their own personal interests, not those of the Lord. In other words, they were motivated by their love for self, not love for the Lord Jesus and His church.

Okay, what laws do they break in doing so? One of the greatest commandments on which all others hang, according to the Lord Jesus Himself: "'You shall love the Lord your God with all your heart, with all your soul, and with all your mind.' This is the first and great commandment. And the second is like it: 'You shall love your neighbor as yourself.' On these two commandments hang all the Law and the Prophets" (Matthew 22:37-40 NKJV).

The key word in this passage is "all." The earlier chapters of this book conveyed the necessity of the believer's exclusive agape love for Jesus as a necessary condition for salvation—that is what believing means in John 3:16.

Now, making money honestly with one's hard work, empowered by the Lord's blessing, is not sinful in itself, but there is great danger for Christians who are consumed by the quest for earthly riches, and for good reasons. The Lord Jesus warns us against such pursuits because the human heart engaged in such a quest becomes divided and even strays away from God (Matthew 6:19-24).

We may find all sorts of arguments to reason that such a thing will never happen to us because we are serving or creating wealth to serve God. Such reasoning is even more likely among ministers who have somehow convinced themselves that they are entitled to earthly riches because they are doing God's work. That is either ignorance or a self-deceiving lie.

The Lord Himself tells us in Matthew 6:24 that no one can be fully devoted to two masters at the same time. The greatest of the commandments, as quoted above, does not leave room for the believer's heart to be divided between God and some other overriding personal interest. There is no biblical basis for a believer to use Christian ministry as a means to realize his or her financial ambitions. True Christian ministry is a calling; it is neither a profession nor an activity designed for personal gain.

Many will be quick to point to Deuteronomy 25:4 as the basis for the biblical principle that justifies such use of Christian ministry, and I quote: "You shall not muzzle an ox while it treads out the grain" (NKJV). However, even a cursory analysis of the passage reveals otherwise. We all agree that the principle of this passage clearly conveys that the full-time minister's immediate needs must be met while he or she is doing the work of ministry. Like the needs of the ox treading out the grain, the full-time minister's needs must be met while his or her time is dedicated to the work of ministry. Those who facilitate such ministries are promised to be rewarded as much as the minister(s) they support (Matthew 10:41).

What is hard to explain is how we leap from meeting the minister's needs to the minister commanding a salary, or to the minister's entitlement to exceedingly luxurious lifestyles, while most of the people paying for that lifestyle live in poverty.

114

Note that Deuteronomy 25:4 neither says to set aside a predetermined portion of grain for the oxen, nor does it command any luxurious accommodations for the yoked oxen who could only eat the grain that falls within reach. Have you ever wondered why God established the tithes and offerings as means to provide for the Levites instead of a salary? Perhaps He did so because He knew that in their minds, the money would quickly supersede their calling as servants in the Lord's house and become the primary reason for the work they performed. Thus, in their minds, they would start to serve the gift rather than continue to serve the Giver.

In spite of God's abundant provision for the Levites, they still ended up devising ways to exploit the children of Israel. The same thing is happening today in the churches. The tithes and offerings, which are the means established by God to provide for those engaged in full-time ministry, have become a way for ministers to exploit the believers. The so-called spiritual gifts meant to edify the church have become the means by which believers are exploited! No wonder the Lord Jesus says in Matthew 6:22, "The eye is the lamp of the body. If your eyes are healthy, your whole body will be full of light. But if your eyes are unhealthy, your whole body will be full of darkness. If then the light within you is darkness, how great is that darkness!" (NKJV).

The poverty-stricken congregants are taught that they are poor due to not having a harvest to reap because they have not sown any seeds. They are told that sowing the seeds of financial prosperity means giving to God. And what is a better way to give to God than to directly or indirectly fill the treasury of the church, or in some cases, the bank accounts of the minister, with money the believers don't have? Some preachers go as far as teaching that the way to financial prosperity is to establish covenants with God, where the believer who gives the most would be guaranteed to obtain the highest return on their gift! Others even create giving competitions among the congregants, spurring them on to go above and beyond their means to give to the church, and the list of schemes goes on.

Please don't misunderstand my statements regarding this issue of the quest for financial gain via Christian ministry. I have been paying my tithes for the last thirty-two years. I have personally supported and continue to financially support several missionaries around the world. I have significantly contributed and continue to contribute to the construction of several church buildings at home and abroad. My point is that I believe in unwavering support for those engaged in Christian ministry. What I do not condone is the use of Christian ministry to exploit God's people! And I have seen, and continue to see, my share of that practice in Africa, America, and around the world to this day.

I first saw the practice in full swing during a personal journey to Africa in 2012, when I was invited to attend a church service one Sunday morning. About one hour into the service, the preacher started his sermon, where he relentlessly touted his message of prosperity for all who sow seeds. At the end of the sermon, he told the congregants that whosoever wishes to be blessed a hundredfold must approach the altar with the seeds they want to sow.

I was utterly saddened to see the congregants press against each other to get closer to the pulpit to offer their envelopes. By their appearances, I could not help but notice that the majority of those seeking the hundredfold blessings were visibly poor mothers who could barely afford a full meal for their children daily. They were being deceived by a preacher who drove a Mercedes-Benz 340 series while his congregants were living in poverty.

Many thought that he was doing the work of God, but I was disturbed in my spirit! No one can fully serve two masters, and performing ministry in interests other than the Lord's is lawlessness because such work is done with a divided heart and mind.

At this point, you must be wondering what the true Christian ministry is. In other words, what is ministry approved by the Lord Jesus Christ? Let's shift our attention to an examination of the concept in light of relevant Scriptures.

Effective Christian Ministry
First, Christian ministry is work that is motivated by the minister's love for Christ and His church, whereas secular work is motivated by the personal interests and ambitions of the worker. Secondly, the ultimate goal of secular work is to satisfy the personal fleshly desires of the worker, such as putting food on the table, gathering material goods, making money, and achieving social status or fame.

These desires are motivated by love for self, and getting the job done is the ultimate objective of any related activities. In contrast, the ultimate goal of Christian ministry, as stated in 2 Corinthians 2:17, is the growth of Christians to the full knowledge of Christ—a spiritual and selfless goal. Unlike the secular business arena, getting the job done cannot be the objective of any activity in Christian ministry. The Christian minister performs physical work with the paramount objective of obtaining spiritual results beyond the visible work products, and only the Holy Spirit can produce such results via the appropriate spiritual gifts. Thus, Christian ministry requires the power of God to achieve its objectives, not wise persuasive words anchored in human wisdom or secular skills (1 Corinthians 2:4-5).

Any work powered by someone's natural abilities is not genuine Christian ministry. It is devoid of the power of the Holy Spirit and, therefore, cannot bear any spiritual fruit (John 15:5). It is no wonder that most of today's ministries are spiritually fruitless. The vast majority of Christians have been attending churches for decades without experiencing any noticeable spiritual growth. Church programs are being conducted and related activities are being performed week after week, month after month, year after year, even decade after decade, with almost no spiritual impact on the congregants or the world!

Let me demonstrate with some practical examples. Does your church seek spiritually gifted people when hiring for an open ministry position? Does it consider spiritual satiety—the state of being Spirit-filled—as a criterion while appointing worship leaders, treasurers, finance committee members, Sunday School teachers, nursery workers, deacons, elders, church secretaries, maintenance staff members, and even pastors? If so, praise the Lord for your church; most churches fail to do so! Why is that? Don't these ministry positions all have an impact on the edification of those who attend the churches? Doesn't natural wisdom even tell us that a job is better done by a qualified and trained worker? Why do churches neglect the most fundamental qualification that their ministers should possess?

There are two main reasons for that: it is either done out of pure ignorance or motivated by personal agendas. On the one hand, churches with leaders who either lack discernment for spiritual gifts or are ignorant of the paramount importance of spiritual gifts cannot recognize or prioritize these when hiring or appointing ministers. On the other hand, church leaders with personal agendas prioritize their personal objectives over the Christian's growth to the full knowledge of Christ. What matters to them above all is completing the tasks at hand, and that is typically accomplished without regard to how it gets done. So, the tendency is to rely on business practices to run a Christian ministry. Yes, getting the job done brings in members by the dozens, by the hundreds, and sometimes by the thousands; it brings in financial gifts and offerings by the thousands and sometimes by the millions of dollars. Thus, we have mega churches with thousands, hundreds of thousands, and sometimes millions of members!

Ministers are enriched and become multimillionaires. They own personal jets and opulent possessions but attribute them to the church in order to avoid paying the related ownership taxes, a scheme that makes them even richer.

In view of all those visible results, we are impressed! We consider such churches very successful. They are certainly successful businesses! However, their success as churches quickly dims when we start to do an inventory of the spiritual maturity of those who lead or attend those churches. Sadly, we find out that most professing Christians don't even know what they say they believe. They have no idea how to live out what they say they believe. There is barely, if at all, any difference between their way of life and that of the unbeliever. Their marriages are in shambles; their children are "raised in the church" but are turned off by the hypocrisy evident in their parents' lives; they do not want anything to do with Christianity. Divorces are rampant in the churches. The leaders of the churches are marred with sexual scandals disguised under the term "moral failures!"

It is clear that we have been using the wrong criteria to measure success in this context. I think that the Lord Jesus would prefer to have a few true and mature believers than thousands of lost souls sitting in churches and thinking that they are believers when, in reality, they have all been misled and are truly lost.

This is a harsh and hard-to-swallow reality, so you might argue that only God knows whether those people are saved or not. Perhaps your point is well taken, or is it? How could such people possibly be saved unless they believe in Christ? How can they believe unless they have heard the truth and made a conscientious decision to follow Christ? And how could they have heard the truth unless it was preached to them? How many of today's preachers prioritize preaching the truth of the gospel as written in the Scriptures? Very few, if any! The personal agendas of the preachers have superseded the original purpose of preaching the truth of the gospel to lead souls to believe in the Son of God.

Some preachers dare not speak the truth because they are employees of the church, and the truth might upset some big donors who might leave the church, jeopardizing the lucrative sources of income for its ministers. Others deceive the masses, preaching their "get rich formula" disguised as revelations from God.

Only the Lord knows their motivations, but to those believers who are falling for the schemes of those wolves in sheep's clothing, I ask: have you ever wondered why most of the apostles of Jesus Christ were poor? If there indeed exist "get rich formulae" for all Christians, how come Jesus didn't teach any to His disciples, whom He called friends, and to whom He revealed the mysteries of God concerning the most important matter in a human life: God's plan for the salvation of mankind? Is it because Jesus did not know the formulae, or did He not love His apostles enough to alleviate their suffering from poverty? No! That is impossible: He was willing to die an egregious death on a Roman cross for them. Sharing such knowledge with them would have been a small matter, but He didn't. By the way, Jesus Himself was not rich while He was on Earth (Matthew 8:20).

Perhaps there exists no "get rich formula" after all. Perhaps the "prosperity gospel" is nothing but a christening of the schemes invented by many in the business community and disguised as financial prosperity training programs to enrich themselves to the detriment of their weak, naïve, or ignorant neighbors.

My point is that God deals with individuals based on their personal characters and as He sees fit, the same way the Lord Jesus deals with the seven churches in the book of Revelation, chapters 1–3. He allows some individuals to acquire riches and others to remain without, but He cares for the least of His creatures; needless to say, He cares for us all (Matthew 6:25-32). His priority is our spiritual prosperity, not earthly riches (Matthew 6:32).

This is not to say that the Lord wants His children to suffer in poverty. Just like any other source of suffering experienced by humans in this world, poverty is mostly a result of the sin of mankind: Adam literally lacked nothing until he chose to go against God's will and was chased out of the garden of Eden, where he had been enjoying everything with Eve, his wife. As such, poverty sometimes indirectly results from the sinful and oppressive practices of economic actors. Other times, it directly results from the bad choices that people make while exercising their God-given free will.

Making better choices is not promised to make one rich, but it goes a long way to support the Lord's plan to provide for us. The Lord does not force anyone into His plans for humanity because He chose to endow mankind with the privilege of free will from creation, but

I digress; let's get back to the topic of Christian ministry for some final remarks.

Until the churches start to make applicable spiritual gifts compulsory criteria in the appointments of their ministers, they will continue to spin their wheels without any significant spiritual results concerning the maturity of the congregants. Hiring professional ministers primarily based on their training in Bible schools will not yield the expected spiritual results. No amount of such schooling can teach anyone the knowledge of Christ, which can only be acquired by experience through a personal relationship with Him.

It is not about knowing about Christ; it is about knowing Him as a person; there is a huge difference. Those with knowledge about Christ perform without any spiritual impact, often leaning on business-based human wisdom to attract the masses. Those who know Christ and are spiritually gifted achieve spiritual results through the power of the Spirit. They make converts who believe in God's power, not in idealized human ministers.

CHAPTER 11

The Achilles Heel

"You shall love your neighbor as yourself"
(Matthew 22:37-40 NKJV).

I expect most casual readers to start reading this chapter and give up quickly because of the heart-wrenching truth that will soon be exposed to their conscience. It pains me greatly to bring these truths to light, but my love for my neighbor compels me to do so.

The brutal truth is that the majority of those labeled today as followers of Christ could not be deceived any more than they currently are. Please understand that I am not arguing and cannot argue against the deeds of most modern-day Christians. They claim to have been "saved"; they profess Christ. Some are preachers; many lead worship, Bible studies, prayer groups, Sunday school, and many more church programs that we do not have space to enumerate in this chapter. All is done in the name of Christ, or so they believe.

Some have taken up the devotion to feed the hungry, shelter the homeless, and rescue the vulnerable from the evil deeds of human trafficking, etc. There is no shortage of missions and ministries in the church today, and that is very commendable!

Unfortunately, these deeds are mostly done out of self-fulfillment, or so it seems; let me explain. All of the above deeds testify to the doers' love for the Lord and the neighbor, or do they? Do we send missionaries around the world because we love those to whom they are being sent? Or are we doing our so-called "work for the Lord"? This is an outrageous affirmation; yet, we cannot ignore the "elephant in the room" and continue to pretend that we are in the truth.

The racial divide in the church today is a convicting prosecution of the motivations fueling our deeds. You are probably exempting your own deeds from the above scrutiny, perhaps arguing that indeed they are committed out of love for Christ and the neighbor, and you would be right if only you could answer these questions in the affirmative. Would you receive, with open arms, another follower of Christ from a different country? What about one of your own countrymen from a different race? Would you entertain a brotherly relationship with such an individual? Would you treat them like you would your siblings? Would you give your son or daughter in marriage to such a believer out of love for Christ and His beloved? Would you not treat them differently in any way because they are not from your culture or because the Lord chose to give them a skin color other than your own? Would you be able to relate to them on the grounds of brotherly Christian love?

If we fail to answer these questions with an affirmative yes, how can we claim that we are doing all the missions and church programs because we love those to whom we are ministering? Perhaps we do not realize the importance of love for our Christian brother? It is one of the main themes that preoccupied Jesus Christ while He was on Earth; it is so important that even He, Christ Jesus, prayed for it! I dare say that the Lord knew that the lack of love for God and the brother or sister is the Achilles' heel of those who want to follow Him. Why? Because He judges our love for Himself by our commitment to truly love our brother and neighbor.

Through the story of the Good Samaritan, the Lord unequivocally teaches us who our neighbor is. It includes all of our loved ones, all those we do not like, and yes, even our most heinous enemies (Matthew 5:44). Our love for the Lord is not measured by how much we do "for Him"; it is measured by our commitment to keep (obey) His commands: "He who has My commandments and keeps them, it is he who loves Me. And he who loves Me will be loved by My Father, and I will love him and manifest Myself to him," said the Lord in John 14:21 NKJV. He is the one who commands us to love our brother and neighbor. We demonstrate our love for Him by doing so.

If you are a prospective churchgoer or someone who has bought into the diluted teachings prevalent in modern-day Christian circles, you may be thinking that my words in this chapter portray Christianity in ways that are the total opposite of what it is supposed to be; that is because Christianity really is so. Consider what the Lord Jesus conveys to His followers in Luke 14:26-33. He is saying that one wanting to be His follower (a Christian) must think hard about the drastic changes in lifestyle that are to be made. Becoming a Christian is a life-changing decision that is not to be taken lightly. It is about a commitment to obey regardless of the consequences.

In the early 2000s, my family relocated from the state of Ohio to New Jersey. As a result, it became necessary for us to obtain new driver's licenses within a couple of months of our relocation date. By the way, if you think that your local DMV office is inefficient, it is nothing compared to that of Paramus, New Jersey, in those days. That office had a telephone number without an automated answering service or a live agent to serve the public. The popular DMV websites did not exist at that time. The only way to obtain any information from the Paramus DMV office was to drive there and stand in a long line for at least 45 minutes just to learn about the process of getting a New Jersey driver's license.

To make the situation more frustrating, there was no written listing of the documents necessary to complete the process. Depending on the specific case of the customer seeking such a driver's license, the clerk at the counter would verbally list the needed documents. Needless to say, the clerk could not always provide the complete list of documents pertaining to a case unless he or she knew the specific circumstances surrounding the customer's application for a new driver's license. So, newcomers like us had to make several trips to the office, which was over 10 miles away, before getting the set of required documents in order.

While returning from one of those trips, we had to stop on a busy street in downtown Englewood, where one could only park head-in on lots diagonal to the street. I was able to successfully park my car next to a relatively expensive Acura sedan. When it was time to leave, I started to back out of the parking space, with my full attention on the bidirectional traffic passing behind while taking quick looks at the front of my car, as a good driver would normally do. In a split second, I heard a rubbing noise and immediately stopped: the front bumper of my car had just scratched the rear passenger side of the parked Acura sedan, leaving my own car's side signal light shattered but functional.

The owner of the damaged vehicle was nowhere to be found, and the impact was so subtle that no other person besides me seemed to have realized what had just happened. In fact, I could have just left, and no one would have noticed anything out of the ordinary, but I knew I had damaged someone's property, and were I in the owner's shoes, I would not want the person responsible for the damages to disappear without saying anything. I also knew that it would cost me quite a bit of money to repair the damaged vehicle, whether through an insurance claim or otherwise. Nevertheless, I did not hesitate for a second to make the decision to wait for the owner of the damaged vehicle to eventually show up.

Surely, the owner did show up after 20 to 30 minutes of waiting; she was a middle-aged lady who was not going to speak to me in spite of my repeated shouting, "Excuse me! Excuse me!" to get her attention. She proceeded to get into her car via the driver's side door and was ready to drive away. So, I walked up to the car and knocked on the raised front driver's side window. She stopped and lowered the window. I explained to her what had happened, showed her the damage, and offered to repair her car. To my surprise, she started to panic and would not speak to me any further without the police, so I called them.

The police officer arrived, and after examining the damage, advised us to settle the matter without filing a formal claim to avoid premium hikes on our respective insurance policies. The lady declined the officer's proposal and insisted on establishing a formal report and insurance claim due to the lack of confidence that I would keep my promise to repair her car. I gently reminded her that I would have left the area or let her leave without telling her about the accident if I were going to flee from my responsibilities.

The officer, who was attentively listening to the conversation, was utterly astonished to hear that I was the one who had insisted on bringing the accident to the lady's attention. He literally asked me, "Did you really do that?"
"Yes," I answered.

The lady also confirmed my answer.

The officer turned to me and said, "Thank God, there are still some good people around!"

Hearing that, the lady realized I was not about to flee from my responsibility to repair her car. I advised her to take it to the dealer, and I would pay for the cost of the repairs. Thus, we exchanged contact information, agreed on how to proceed with the repairs, and went to our respective homes. That night, I received a call from the lady's husband thanking me for how I handled what had happened. He was a Christian brother and suspected that I would be as well, so he called me. A couple of weeks later, I paid $500 for the repairs of the lady's car, and the matter was settled.

I must acknowledge that this was not a matter of life and death; however, it entailed real consequences for me and my family, given the economic climate prevailing in the tri-state area of the Eastern coast of the United States during the early 2000s and the expenses that our family had just incurred to relocate to a new state.

My point is that obedience calls for willingness to comply in every circumstance, big or small, even when no other human is watching—the Lord is always watching. Loving one's neighbor is often costly, but it is inherent to the godly integrity required to follow Christ. The good news is that "our present sufferings are not worth comparing with the glory that will be revealed in us" (Romans 8:18 NIV) when the Lord returns to Earth and the elect are glorified.

Getting back to our main topic of interest in this chapter, I must say that I am appalled by the deafening silence of those in the pulpit concerning the apparent absence of biblical love for God and the neighbor within today's church congregations. That silence is literally robbing those who would otherwise seek true conversion to Christianity of their lifetime opportunity to live for Christ. Indeed, many run the risk of a heartbreaking experience when they stand before the Lord, attempting to account for all they have done in His name, only to hear Him say, "I never knew you: depart from me" (Matthew 7:23 NKJV).

Some readers may be thinking that the above-referenced passage is about those who did not profess Christ in their lifetime; nothing could be farther from the truth. Note that those making the claims of great accomplishments in the name of the Lord did indeed do the things they are claiming.

The all-knowing Lord does not call them liars because they are telling the truth. He instead rejects them for being practitioners of lawlessness. Of course, this is about divine law as taught by the Scriptures. I am not speaking about the Ten Commandments as given to Moses; I am talking about the spirit of all the commandments, which the Lord Jesus summed up for us in these words: "You shall love the Lord your God with all your heart, with all your soul, and with all your mind. This is the first and great commandment. And the second is like it: 'You shall love your neighbor as yourself. On these two commandments hang all the Law and the Prophets" (Matthew 22:37-40 NKJV).

The point is that nothing matters to the Lord if we are not committed to obeying His Word. Note that I am not saying, "Nothing matters if we fail to obey divine law." True Christians, not those who claim to be, are not perfect. They still fail to live up to God's perfect standards—often against their own desires, dragged down by the fallen nature of humanity—but they do not practice lawlessness. That is, they love God; they love their neighbors, even their enemies, in the way commanded in Matthew 22:37-40. After we know the truth, we are judged by our commitment to obey, not how well we compensate for our continued disobedience.

Consider King David; he committed sins that most of us will never have the misfortune to commit. Yet, he gained God's heart because of his commitment to repentance and the pursuit of obedience to God at all costs. The Scriptures testify to that through the many times that God extended His mercy to Israel, saying, "For the sake of My servant David."

The church is quenching the Holy Spirit of God by its continued disobedience to God's law of love. If you have been wondering why fewer and fewer people among the younger generations are interested in Christianity, look no further than the church itself. It did not teach the older generations to prioritize living for Christ. Secularism taught them to live for the American Dream. They bought into Satan's lies about raising children and sent both parents to corporate America to make money, abandoning the children to be raised by daycares, nannies, school teachers, and church programs. There is absolutely no biblical foundation or precedent for such transformations of the Christian family.

The Bible makes it crystal clear: it is the parents' responsibility to bring up the child in the ways of God, not the church, not schools, not daycares or nannies. In fact, I will go as far as to say that God's primary interest in the Christian family is to have and raise godly children (Malachi 2:15).

Resuming our discourse concerning love for the brother, sister, and neighbor, secular society is condemning the church with its bold actions to build and integrate a better society for everyone, regardless of country of origin, creed, race, or skin color. It is truly heartbreaking to realize that those who claim to have decided to live according to the model of Jesus Christ, the ultimate lover of humanity, have become entrenched in their own ungodly ways, so much so that pastors dare not speak against the status quo for fear of losing favor with their employers. As a result, the church is one of the most segregated institutions. It is segregated along social classes, races, ethnic groups, to name a few of the criteria. Segregation has become so entrenched in the church that churchgoers have no problem referring newcomers whom they judge unfit for their congregations to others of like social class, race, or ethnic group.

Some factions within those congregations conduct covert Bible studies where they only invite those deemed worthy of association and fellowship. The leaders of those congregations know all about those practices in their churches but dare not speak against them. What we should all realize is that "to whom much is given, much is required." Ignoring the truth for fear of man is shortsighted. The Almighty, who can kill the body and send the soul to hell, is the one to be feared. That is what the Lord Jesus taught in Matthew 10:28.

Much energy and resources are devoted to deeds that will not matter in the end unless we repent, change our ways, and commit to obeying the words of Christ. We will not see the power of God manifest in our lives, nor will the church truly experience the power of the Spirit, until there is repentance.

CONCLUSION

Christianity is all about training the heart, soul, and mind of believers; yet, much of today's church's energy and resources are devoted to deeds that will not matter in the end unless we repent, change our ways, and commit to obeying the words of Christ. To use a sports analogy, the Scriptures are the training instructions; God's Holy Spirit is the coach, and the believers are the players in training.

Unfortunately, the players are not listening to or following the directives of the coach; instead, their captains—church leaders—have established their own agendas and devised their own methods to control the behavior of the players—congregants—for their own benefit. Such human methods may be effective tools to achieve the leaders' personal objectives, but they are spiritually vain exercises.

Man ascribes importance to outward appearances, but the Lord looks at the heart. No outward conditioning regimen will ever amount to sanctification; only the renewing of the believer's mind predicated on the hearing of biblical truth and the cleansing power of the Holy Spirit can sanctify. Behavior control is the antithesis of God's original intent: His desire was to create a being like Himself, one who would also be capable of love, just like He is: mankind. The purity of God's nature would not permit the substitution of the true love that He desired from His new creature for the inherent compliance of a robotic being.

Indeed, love cannot exist in such a being that has no capability of choosing to do otherwise than to comply. Love is only pure and meaningful if it is freely given by the lover. So God created man as a totally free agent, choosing not to interfere with his choice to obey or disobey Him.

On the one hand, He knew that some humans would love Him, whereas others would literally hate Him. He is God. He can take it. On the other hand, He is so just that His nature cannot accept "sweeping any wrongdoing under the rug," to let it go without a penalty paid to right the wrong. Thus, He knew that He would punish man's wrongdoings from the beginning. However, His infinitely loving nature motivated Him to make a way for the penalty of man's wrongdoings to be paid for. He chose the sacrificial death of His Son Jesus Christ on a Roman cross as the only payment worthy to expunge the death penalty deserved by man for his wrongdoings—justification. This was an integral part of the divine plan from the beginning, even before man's disobedience to God—sin.

God also knew that the divine image that He gave man at creation would be tarnished once he disobeyed Him. Man was enticed into disobeying God and has never been able to physically return to the God-like state that was given to him at creation. So, God established a process to start his restoration—sanctification. He sent His Son as the perfect human example and His Holy Spirit to teach and train man's heart, soul, and mind in living like His Son until such a time as He—God—will restore those who believe in the Son to His full likeness—glorification.

Should there be any hope for revival, we must cease to resort to human ingenuity and secular business practices in spiritual matters, fearlessly preach the truth, and believe in the Lord enough to take Him at His word. Until then, churches as they exist today will continue to be mere businesses with a semblance of spirituality, and the attempts to lead the hearts of future generations to the Lord will continue to falter.

References

Youssef, Nagy A., et al. "The Effects of Trauma, with or without PTSD, on Transgenerational DNA Methylation Alterations in Human Offsprings." *Brain Sciences* 8, no. 5 (May 2018): 83. https://doi.org/10.3390/brainsci8050083.

Orr, James, M.A., D.D., ed. *International Standard Bible Encyclopedia.* 1915. Entry for "God, Image of." https://www.studylight.org/encyclopedias/isb/g/god-image-of.html.

Harper, Douglas. *Online Etymology Dictionary.* Accessed August 31, 2025. https://www.etymonline.com/.

www.ingramcontent.com/pod-product-compliance
Lightning Source LLC
Chambersburg PA
CBHW051529120626
46551CB00012B/1150